To Ruby Esti___

Bonnie Heple___

Y0-ARD-878

THE POWER OF LOVE

The POWER *of* LOVE

D. L. DYKES, JR.

ABINGDON PRESS

Nashville

THE POWER OF LOVE

This book is printed on acid-free paper.

Library of Congress Cataloging-in-Publication Data

DYKES, D. L., 1917–
    The power of love / D.L. Dykes, Jr.
        p.   cm.
    ISBN 0-687-33205-2 (alk. paper)
    1. Sermons, American. 2. Methodist Church—Sermons. I. Title.
    BX8333.D95P68   1988   88-19047
    241'.4—dc19   CIP

Most Scripture quotations are from the authorized King James Version of
the Bible; some are the author's own interpretation of Scripture.

"Myself," p. 46, is from *The Collected Verse of Edgar A. Guest,* © 1934 by
Contemporary Books, Inc., used with permission of Contemporary Books,
Inc., Chicago.

MANUFACTURED BY THE PARTHENON PRESS
NASHVILLE, TENNESSEE, UNITED STATES OF AMERICA

*To Sue, who has taught me the
true meaning and power of love*

FROM THE THIRTEENTH CHAPTER
OF THE APOSTLE PAUL'S
FIRST LETTER TO THE CORINTHIANS

Though I speak with the tongues of men and of angels, and have not love, I am become as sounding brass, or a tinkling cymbal.

And though I have the gift of prophecy, and understand all mysteries, and all knowledge; and though I have all faith, so that I could remove mountains, and have not love, I am nothing.

And though I bestow all my goods to feed the poor, and though I give my body to be burned, and have not love, it profiteth me nothing.

Love is patient and kind; love is not jealous or boastful.

Love does not insist on its own way, is not irritable or resentful;

Rejoices not in iniquity, but rejoices in the truth;
Bears all things, believes all things, hopes all things, endures all things.

Love never fails.

CONTENTS

INTRODUCTION

Occasionally in the past, I have been asked, "If you had only one sermon to preach, what would it be?"

Immediately, there always flashed through my mind only one subject, and that is *love*—unconditional love, the kind of love the New Testament calls *agape*, uniquely and graphically demonstrated in the life of Jesus.

This one concept is the "whole" of the Christian faith and the only hope of the world, from the most personal and family relationships to national and international affairs.

The greatest moment in my life took place on October 28, 1956, when I realized the tremendous truth and meaning of a passage I had read so many times before—*"love never fails."*

The sermons contained in this book are thoughts that came out of that moment of realization. They are printed just as they were recorded live, with a minimum of editing.

I have so often failed, but my sincere hope is that God will bless you with the same peace and power that have always come to me, the few times I have practiced what I preached.

THE POWER OF LOVE

W e are a people who live in a time almost totally dedicated to the concept of power. We love *power*. If we are to believe the television commercials, we even want our detergents to have "bulldozer power." We want automobiles with 400-horsepower engines, capable of cruising at 120 miles an hour, when we know we have to drive in zones from 35 to 65 miles an hour. For the most part, our greatest sense of security is in believing that we are the strongest nation in the world. We have the greatest military might in the world, and we can sleep peacefully at night because of that sense of security. *Power* is a watchword of our time.

The meaning of the word can differ according to who is talking. If a wrestling promoter says, "He's a powerful man," he is probably talking about muscle power to crush the bones of an opponent. If a politician says, "He's a powerful man," he is probably talking about power to influence people and get the votes. If a moralist talks about a person with power, he is probably talking about an individual's ability to stand for a principle against the crowd. The meaning of the word *power* can differ according to who is using it at the time.

The meaning can also differ according to what you want to accomplish. If you want to destroy a city, a nuclear bomb is power; if you want to plow a field, a big ox or a tractor is power; but if you want to paint a sunset or write a symphony, then those things are not power. If you want to threaten and intimidate a person or hurt his feelings, then sarcasm and profanity or a gun may be power. But if you want to make a person your friend, then those things are not power.

So the meaning of the word *power* can differ according to who is using it at the time and what they want to accomplish, or what their goal is. Now the big questions: Is there a *power* above all other powers? Is there a kind of power before which all other kinds of power will eventually bow? Is there a *pure power* that doesn't depend on who is talking about it at the time or what they want to accomplish? Is there a kind of power that people who seek any other kind of power are really looking for, even though they may not know it? Is there a kind of power that even the politician, who seeks to get more and more control over more and more people, is really looking for?

Is there a kind of power that even a young boy is looking for—the boy who gets in his sports car with the low-swung bucket seats so he can feel the road beneath him and goes out on the freeway and revs it up to 120 miles an hour, just to feel that surge of power? Is there a different kind of power he is looking for even though he does not know it? Is there a kind of power that will ultimately defeat all other kinds of power? I believe there is.

When I went to seminary, one of the first things they taught us was the attributes of God—that is, the characteristics of God. One of those attributes is *omnipotence*—*God is all power*. In Sunday school, when we had to begin memorizing Scripture, one of the first verses we learned was, *"God is love."* In our college logic course we were taught a principle: When two things are equal to the same thing, they are equal to each other. God is all power; God is love; therefore, *love is all power*.

Now this is what is hard for us to believe. We can believe that love is sweet, that it is nice, that it is advisable, that it is preferable—but not that it is powerful. Even though we may believe it would be better to have love, more advisable to have love; when our backs are against the wall and we need to get things done, we believe we had better find another tool. Down deep in our souls most of us believe it. In fact, the characteristics of love seem at times to be points of weakness—forgiveness, patience, long-suffering, refusal to resist. Under certain kinds of pressure, these seem not to be signs of strength, but marks of weakness.

I believe the day will come when Christian love, the kind of love we are talking about, will ultimately be victorious over all other kinds of love and will prove not only that it is nice, sweet, advisable, and preferable, but that it is pure power.

It is a certain kind of love; it is unconditional. Our forebears called it *grace*—the unmerited favor of God, the undeserved love of God, unconditional love. It has been only in recent years that I have known about this. I don't know how I missed it for so long. Nearly four thousand times, I've stood at an altar somewhere and heard this age-old vow:

"I, Jim, take thee, Mary, to be my wedded wife, to have and to hold from this day forward, for better or worse, richer or poorer, in sickness and in health, to love and to cherish, until death parts us."

This old vow is trying to say, "I take you unconditionally. I am going to love you no matter what you do. I do not take you until you come in drunk or stay out all night or are unfaithful to me. I'm going to love you, no matter what you do. I take you unconditionally." That's what this old vow is trying to say, and this is the kind of love we are talking about—that is pure power.

First of all, *love is more powerful than force of any kind*. If you have a child and your control over your child is based on force, then you will have control over your child only as long as that child is at home with you, where you can monitor behavior and the child is physically small enough for you to control. When that child gets old enough to move away to a dormitory on a college campus somewhere or into an apartment complex in a distant city or just gets big enough to stand up in the middle of the room and tell you "No," then you don't have any control over your child—if that control has been based on force. But if your control has been based on love, then that child can move to any college dormitory anywhere, or to any apartment in any city, or get to weigh 240 pounds, and your control will be just the same as when he was a little boy and she was a little girl, swinging their feet under the dinner table.

Who is the person who has the greatest control over me? It is not the person who threatens me with force. In fact, I'm the kind of person who, if someone tries to threaten me with force, I tend to want to do the opposite. The person who has the greatest power over me is the person who, for more than forty years, has proved to me that she is going to love me no matter what I do or how I speak to her or how I act. Through the years when I've been away somewhere, maybe tempted to be less than my best, that face comes up before me. This is the person who controls me.

Napoleon, on one occasion, said, "God is on the side of the ones who have the biggest guns." Napoleon was mistaken. One of these days some nation is going to take its stand with love, unilaterally. It is going to say that it disavows force as a method of solving the problems of the world on an international basis.

My wife, Sue, and I saw the movie *Gandhi*. I sat there, and for the only time in my life, I felt a holy hush in a theater. God was present in that theater. Gandhi's stand was, "I won't fight you, but I won't do what you say. I won't do as you tell me to do but I am going to love you. If you shoot me, then you'll just have to shoot me . . . I'm not going to shoot you. This is where I stand; I stand here, live or die, and I am going to love you, live or die." The British didn't know what to do with him. By the sheer power of unconditional love, he almost single-handedly defeated the British Empire in the Far East, when armies for generations had never been able to do it. Of course, that nation did it because it seemed to be the only thing it could do; it couldn't accomplish anything militarily.

But one of these days some nation that could do it militarily is going to take its stand with love. If and when this happens, people of every color and kind and creed across the face of the earth are going to gravitate to that nation as if to a holy mountain. The world is starving to death for this, and that nation is going to rule the hearts and minds of everyone across the face of the earth. There is no power on earth like the power of love, and some day even nations are going to know this.

Second, *love is more powerful than persuasion*. Not only is it more powerful than force; it is more powerful than persuasion. Many of us, when we decide we can't force people to do what we think they ought to do, decide that we can win them by persuasion or by argument. But for every person who has been argued into the kingdom of heaven, a thousand have been loved into it.

Dr. Nat Long, when he was pastor a good many years ago of that great Glenn Memorial Church, on the campus of Emory University in Atlanta, one day told a group of ministers this story. He said that one Sunday morning he went into the pulpit, and as he looked out into the congregation, there sat a man he was amazed to see. He was one of the biggest industrialists, one of the most powerful businessmen in the city, but he was an avowed atheist and bragged about it at every opportunity. Not only was he there that Sunday, but he showed up the next Sunday, and the next.

Dr. Long said that in his study every week, he found

himself preparing his sermon especially with this man in mind because he felt that if he could somehow convert him, what a power he could be in the community! Sure enough, one Sunday morning when he finished preaching and gave the invitation, that man came out of the pew and down the aisle with tears streaming down his face. He knelt at the altar, professed faith in Christ as his Savior, and joined the church. After the benediction, Dr. Long took his new convert back into the study to visit for a few minutes, and their conversation became rather confidential.

The preacher said to the new convert, "I want to ask you a question. If you can answer it, it might help me to help a lot of other people. Which one of my sermons was it? What idea was the turning point for you, and what started you in the other direction?"

The man said, "Dr. Long, I've enjoyed and appreciated your sermons, and I wouldn't hurt your feelings for anything, but it was none of your sermons. It was the fact that for forty-one years I've lived with two of the kindest, most loving people that God ever made." He said, "I want to be able to love like my wife and daughter love. I want a God in my life like my wife worships."

Every now and then some wife will say to me, "How can I get my husband or my son or my daughter in church, or to be interested in religion?"

I say to them, "Just love them, just love them. Don't argue with them. Don't try to persuade them. You've probably said all you could ever say. If anything will work, it will be to just love them." Love is more powerful than force of any kind, and love is more powerful than persuasion and argument.

Third, *love is more powerful than money.* We, in our culture, tend to believe that if we have enough money we can do anything. Money is power.

One night I was called to a local hospital. The son of a very wealthy, powerful man in our community had had an automobile accident in a sports car and was critically injured. He was still alive when I got there. I was standing outside the operating room with the father when the doctor came out and told him his son was going to die.

The man grabbed the front of the doctor's surgical coat and said, "Doctor, I have enough money to bring any doctor or any surgeon in the world here to save my son." Even in the midst of what he was saying, I could see the expression on his face change as he realized that there are some things you can't buy, no matter how much money you have.

Here are two fathers—one of them is very successful; everything he touches turns to profit. His estate builds and builds. When his children come along, he can give them everything they need, their heart's desire. He can even give them things before they know they want them. As the years pass, he is amazed that he is a failure as a father. He will sit and tell the preacher, "I don't understand my boy. I've given him everything money can buy, and look how he's turned out. He's had everything from the time he can remember, and look at him. He doesn't appreciate anything."

Here is another father; fortune doesn't smile on him. Just when his children are at the age when they need him most, he loses his job. At forty-three years of age, it is hard to get a job. He comes for counseling, and he cries and says, "I'm a failure as a father." He thinks because he can't give his children all these material things, he is a failure. He tries to make up for it by loving them. As the years pass, *he* is amazed that he is a *success* as a father—they all turn out good. Love and everything it accomplishes is more powerful than money.

A man I know has four daughters. We were sitting in my study, and he sat there and cried until his shoulders were shaking. I went around the desk and put my arm around his shoulders and called him by his first name and said, "You are not a failure as a father; you don't owe those girls anything except to love them properly. It is nice that you can give them these other things, but you don't owe them anything except to love them properly, and that you have done." Thank God, they are every one proving it. Love is more powerful than force or persuasion or money.

And finally, *love is more powerful than education.* We tend to say to our young people, "Just get your education, and everything is going to be all right." I wish it were true, and I hope you get your education, but I hate to tell you it is just not so. There is a section of every city where you have to build a house that costs over a half-million dollars in order to get a building permit. Our city has a section like that, and as I drive onto those circular driveways and call on people in those homes, people who have all that education can offer, I realize that some of them live in hell because they don't know how to love.

I have two little granddaughters. They come to our home occasionally for a few days, and every time I sit and watch them, I think to myself, "I'd rather they would learn how to love properly than learn anything else in the world."

If you ask people who are experts in dealing with human nature and human problems, they will tell you that some people have problems not because they don't know how to do their jobs and not because they haven't been trained to do their jobs properly. Those people have trouble throughout their lives because they don't know how to get along with other people, with themselves, and with God. They don't know how to love.

We can't teach God or the Bible in our schools, but we could teach love. Why not have a high school course on love? It is more important than anything else you can learn. You can take two boys—one of them can go away to agricultural school and learn everything about raising plants and cattle. The other boy may not have that opportunity, but he loves the earth. He will come out in the early morning and pick up some of the earth in his hands and feel it, and smell it, and even taste it; and if he has that quality, he will be a success as a farmer.

There have been experiments with the effect of love on plants. At Yale University, researchers have some plants in one room to which they go every morning and talk nicely to them, stroke them, and are friendly with them. They have plants in another room to which they go every morning and fuss at them. The man in charge of this experiment was on the "Johnny Carson Show." He had a big rubber plant there, and he had a console with some little dials on it. There were some electrodes coming out of his console, and he hooked the wires to the leaves of this rubber plant.

He gave Johnny Carson some big shears and said to him, "Now you approach this plant with the intent of cutting it, and let's see what happens."

Johnny clowned around and said to the plant, "I'm going to cut you." The dial didn't move.

The professor said, "Mr. Carson, you are not serious. Get serious. Approach the plant with the intent of cutting it, then cut the plant." Mr. Carson did, and before he even touched the plant, the needle went wild. The power of love apparently affects everything.

We have a wonderful person at our house named Ruth. She has worked for us for more than thirty years. Ruth does not have much formal education, but she is one of the wisest people I have ever known because she knows how to love. Time and time again, when we have gone through some "valley of shadows" in our family, I have walked into the kitchen, and she would be standing at the sink with tears in her eyes—tears of love. Because she loves, she has wisdom; she is smart. Many a time when I have had a problem, I have pulled a stool up by the sink in the kitchen and said, "Ruth, I want to tell you about something and see what you think." Love is more powerful than any amount of education. It is in everything.

I do not know what your problem is today, but if you have one with anybody, and if anything will solve it, love will. Quit trying anything else. If anything will work, love will work.

It just may be that one of these days we will discover that the whole creative life force that put it all here and makes it grow is love. Wouldn't it be something if one of these days we discovered that the power that created the whole universe in the first place—the sun, the moon, the stars, and the planets; and holds them in place and keeps them going—is the power of love!

In the book of Genesis, the first chapter says, "In the beginning God created the heavens and the earth." And what is God? God is love. Therefore, *love* created the heavens and the earth.

I don't know when I have been as moved as when I sat and watched the movie *Gandhi* I mentioned earlier; this little dark-skinned Indian lived as no other man we know about, so close to what Jesus taught. There was a scene in which Gandhi was lying on his bed, and a man came in wild-eyed because he hated the Moslems who had killed his son. He wanted to know what to do to get his sanity back. You could see the insanity of hate in his eyes. Gandhi rolled over on his side and said to him, "My recommendation to you, my friend, is that you go adopt a Moslem child and raise him as a Moslem." Go all the way. Cast your lot totally with love.

Paul never wrote a truer word than when he said in that beautiful thirteenth chapter of First Corinthians, *"Love never fails."* One of these days this world is going to discover this secret, and then the kingdom of heaven will come on earth. That's when it's coming!

PRAYER

O Lord, our heavenly Father, most of us have a problem of some kind, and we keep believing that we are going to find the solution; we are going to be smart enough to solve it; we are going to be able to touch the right button, and all the doors will open. Father, help us today as Christians to rediscover the oldest and most consistent precept of the faith—the power of love—not only to sweeten and enrich life, but to get things done. Father, help us as a nation of people to graduate out of that tragic period when we were willing to use any tool, abandon all morality, in the name of saving ourselves and our people. Let us turn to that one power which ultimately will save us and all humankind—the power of love. For it is in Jesus' name we ask it. Amen.

FIVE WAYS TO EXPRESS LOVE

*T*here is a lot more love in the world than any of us realize. It's bottled up in the hearts of people who don't know how to express it. Now, it's good that the love is there, but it is so sad that it lies dormant and untapped, like a great deposit of precious metal such as gold or uranium. It is so sad that it is wasted, when it is such a tremendous force for happiness and for healing the problems of human relationships in the world. If the love that is already felt in the hearts of people could somehow be expressed, what a tremendous blessing it would be to the world. Knowing how to love is hard enough for all of us; but for many of us, it is even more difficult to know how to *express* the love we already feel.

We still have what is known as the "sensitivity group." These groups are being formed by therapists, ministers, and teachers all over the country. The purpose is to bring together, in small groups of eight or ten, persons who are supposed to relate to one another in total honesty. The most significant accomplishment considered by the leaders of such groups is that people learn how to express openly the hostilities they feel toward one another. It seems to me that what most people need, more than anything else, is not to learn how to express their hostilities. The world is pretty expert at that!

What we need most are some situations in which we can learn, rather, to *express* the love we already feel in our hearts, either for the people who are closest to us or the people we come in contact with incidentally or humankind in general. People are much more expert in expressing their hostilities than they are in expressing their love. In fact, the most unhappy people I ever come in contact with know pretty well how to express their hostilities. Some of them are very expert at it. What they don't know is how to express their love. There is no telling how many husbands and wives lie night after night by the side of a mate, with their hearts so full of love they can hardly contain it, not knowing how to express it . . . hoping for an open door of some kind to encourage them and show them the way to express the love they've never been able to demonstrate.

There is no telling how many mothers and fathers sit and look across a room or around a dinner table at sons or daughters, with hearts so full of love and concern for them that they would give their right arm to be able to openly and truly express and communicate it.

Saint Paul, in his first letter to his friends in the church at Corinth, was describing this great need to know how to express the love that we feel. He was outlining the ways that love can be expressed. Much of the life and teaching of Jesus was dedicated to encouraging people and teaching them how to express the love they feel. Now, what are some of the ways the Christian faith says that we can express love?

First of all, *love can be expressed in touch*. There is tremendous power of communication in the human touch. In fact, there is a quality of love that cannot be expressed *except* in touch. So often when Jesus wanted to transmit the power of his healing love and concern for people, he touched them. In at least one incident in the New Testament, we have a story recorded in which, by the touch of someone, Jesus literally felt that love flow from him, even though he didn't know who touched him. He turned, according to the story, and said, "Who touched me?" He had felt the love proceed from him. The handshake, the kiss, the pat on the back, have such strong expressive implications. I feel truly sorry for the person who, in early life, did not learn how to receive and give the touch of love.

The Menninger Clinic has continuous experiments going on, working with scientifically selected groups of nursing-home patients who are becoming senile. Often groups of young medical students and nurses go and visit these people. Their instruction is to sit with them, take them by the hand, stroke their hands, speak to them softly, and, sometime before they leave their presence, put an arm around them, maybe kiss them on the cheek, and express their concern for them. According to the reports from the Menninger Clinic, in a few weeks the condition of a large percentage of these persons has greatly improved and many are able to return to their homes.

But there was a surprising by-product and a second result of that experiment. Those young doctors and nurses who were participating in the experiment by touching with love and concern the aging people who had withdrawn from communicating with those about them, found that their own spirits were tremendously lifted. With this sense of well-being, they were able to overcome their own depressions and fears and anxieties in the touch of love.

Psychiatrists have been telling us for a long time now that a large percentage of criminally insane or antisocial people are the products of homes in which a baby longed for the touch of love but did not receive it. They were not touched with care and tenderness in the years in which this was important. Now, we know that often when a baby cries in its crib it is not hungry or wet or pricked with a pin. It is lonely, wanting the feel of another human being, and this is the reason that a continuous light pat on the back, just the touch of a person who walks up to the crib and gently pats the baby on the back, will often put the child back to sleep. There is a tremendous power in the communication of the touch of love.

Recently I read that if you want a dog to remain healthy and secure, you need to pet him a little every day. Often people come much nearer to knowing this about their dogs than they do about the other human beings who live in the family with them.

A young doctor was telling me recently that doctors have learned that one of the main reasons some patients—especially seriously ill patients, and particularly terminal cases (with a disfiguring disease)—set up such a strong attachment for the physician is because other people are afraid to touch them and are repelled by their condition. The doctor, however, regularly comes in without fear and with concern and healing touches for them.

Then in the second place, *love can be expressed in words, both spoken and written.* Some time ago a woman was dying in a local hospital, and her three children came in by plane from various parts of the United States. I happened to be present when her eldest son, who had just arrived from California, entered the room. He walked over to the bedside of his aged and dying mother and leaned over and kissed her and then, probably under the impact of the moment of seeing her, he said to her, "Mother, you've been a good mother." And she looked up at him and said, "Son, that's the first time you ever told me." How often we feel a love we do not speak.

Several years ago we had what we called The Forty Days of Love in our church. During the first week, we were all going to write to some person and express our love and appreciation. Two things happened to me that week that I shall not forget. First, I was walking down the street about a block from the church, and I met a man I know very well. He was very active in the church.

He said, "I want to tell you something. When you first talked about this Forty Days of Love thing, I thought it was sort of silly, and I didn't think it was for me. Then," he said, "I got one of those letters the other day. I don't know of anything that's ever affected me like that did. Yesterday I wrote several letters myself."

The following Sunday I was downstairs in one of the Sunday school classes, and another friend came up to me and told me this experience. He went to the post office one day that week, opened his box, took out his mail, and as he was coming down the steps of the building, he was looking through the mail. He noticed that one of the envelopes was addressed to him in handwriting that looked very familiar. He said the more he looked at it, the more it looked like his wife's handwriting and finally, standing there on the steps, he opened it and read it. It said, "Dear Jim, I could not let this week of 'letter writing' pass without writing one to you. I want to tell you how much I've loved you for these thirty years and how much your love means to me and the children."

I could tell, as he told me this, that he will long remember that letter from one whom he sees every day, but who took the occasion to express love in words again. A good way to express love is in words, either spoken or written.

Another way to express love is in gifts. From the beginning, we have sought to express our love with gifts. Even in early chapters of the book of Genesis, we find Cain and Abel bringing gifts to God to express their love. The wise men, when they came to celebrate the birth of Jesus, brought gifts. It's really too bad that the commercial world has so cashed in on this natural human instinct that often the material value of a gift overshadows the true purpose of the expression of love.

A preacher friend of mine told me about a young woman in his congregation who went to a very isolated section of the world as a missionary. The first Christmas, she was in a place where there was no contact with the outside world except a monthly visit by helicopter. It flew over the village in the jungles, dropped food supplies and mail to her, then swooped down and picked up from a clearing the mail and other things she wished to send out.

For Christmas that year her family received a large envelope; she asked that it be put under the Christmas tree. When it was opened on Christmas morning, there was a small envelope addressed to each member of the family and a letter which said, "I am not in a place that I can buy anything to send you as a gift, but I'm sending each of you my gift in this envelope. When you open them, put them together and they are my gift to you." When they opened them, they found that she had taken a large piece of red paper and had cut it into five pieces and put one piece in each envelope to the members of her family. When they put the pieces together, they had her heart.

We need to give simple gifts of love regularly and often—a rose, a flower, a small box of candy, a handkerchief, some little token that expresses the way we feel. It's a good way to express love.

Then in the fourth place, *we can express love with our very facial expressions.* In New Testament days, Jesus was often reported as having great power in the way he looked at people. Again and again the Scriptures say that he looked with compassion or pity or love. In the story of the rich young ruler, "He looked upon him and loved him."

As I look back over my life, the way people have looked at me at times has been a great influence. I can remember how my father used to look at me when we had company and I was misbehaving. I can remember how, in the early days of my ministry, it was even more frightening to go into the pulpit to preach than it is now. Often I would search the congregation for my wife Sue's face, for the reassurance of her look of love. There is a look of love, and it is sometimes a very beautiful way to express it.

And finally, *love can be expressed in action*. There is an old saying that actions speak louder than words, and sometimes this is true. The greatest thing we can do for anyone we love is to be a certain kind of person.

I have talked to young men who have greatly disappointed their parents and hurt them. Some have been repentant and have said, "Dr. Dykes, I love my mother and father very much. How can I let them know?"

I say, "I think the best way to let them know is to behave in a certain way, to become a certain kind of person, to be the kind of person in your actions that they so much want you to be." I suppose the best way to express love is to live it.

PRAYER

O Lord, our Heavenly Father, we are timid about it . . . we admit it. Long ago some of us gave up. How often we have wanted to reach out and touch someone, but we were afraid. We weren't sure what the response would be or we were sure we would do it wrong. How often we have wanted to say how we feel but the words would not come. Many of us have found that for many years we have carried deep love and concerns which we have never expressed. Dear God, help us, that we might be able to express our love. We ask it in the name of him who said to us, "God is love," even Jesus, the Christ. Amen.

TWO WAYS TO LOVE

One Sunday morning while we were at church, someone shot and killed our little dog, Spot. The veterinarian we took him to, and who buried him for us, told us that whoever did it apparently stood directly above him and shot him. The bullet entered his back and went straight through. It was a very sad time for us around the house. It's extremely difficult to understand how a person could do a thing like this.

Now, Spot was not anything unusual as dogs go—he wasn't registered, he was not a thorough-bred—he had no great talents; he never did bring the paper to us and he wasn't a very good watchdog. He was too friendly to be a watchdog; he welcomed everybody. I guess he was glad to see anyone come to the house, even a burglar, but we loved him, and love is often a mixture of joy and pain. It's a beautiful combination of both, and one of the great capacities of the human spirit is to love.

Erich Fromm, that great writer, psychologist, and

philosopher, who wrote that wonderful little book *The Art of Loving*, says that love is the most discussed and the least understood subject on earth. People talk about it, sing about it, write poetry about it, tell stories about it, and understand it less than any other subject.

I want to talk about two kinds of love. Now, if you love the first of these ways, then you are going to be unhappy all your life. You are going to be constantly surprised by new tragedy and new disappointment and disillusionment that will be continuous. If you learn to love the other way, you are always going to be surprised by joy. There are going to be unlimited new horizons of glory in your life if you discover, as a few do, how to love the second way.

The famous Oxford professor and converted atheist C. S. Lewis says there are various shades of both of these, but basically, there are just two kinds of love.

The first is what he calls "need love." This is love born out of some kind of need in the lover, a sense of need within us. It arises out of a feeling of emptiness. We see something in another person that we think will fill our emptiness, or loneliness, or insecurity. This kind of love is a way of getting something we need. Many people who move from one marriage partner to another are motivated by this "need love." When they say, "I don't love him anymore" or "I don't love her anymore," what they are really saying is, "I don't find in him (or her) what I need anymore."

A young woman said to me recently, "Don't I have a right to my own happiness?" And of course she does have a right to her own happiness. The only trouble is that she is basically motivated by "need love," always looking for what she needs in another, and she will never find happiness.

"Need love" always has an ulterior motive. It goes out for the purpose of ultimately coming back again. It is a circle, and if the circle is not completed, then it's deeply disappointing. It gives the person loved in this way a vague feeling of being used. Someone has called this "the Kleenex view of people." It sees people as something disposable, to be used and then cast away.

Now, if you and I are perfectly honest, most of our loving is this kind of love—"need love." We see something in another person we need, and we seek to attach ourselves to them. We see a person who knows something we want to know, and we want to associate with them. I see a person who has influence I need, and I make opportunities to be with him. I see a person who has money and position or power, and so I seek to attach myself to him. I see a car and I want it; or as a young man, I see a girl and I want her. All this is "need love," and the person who loves this way will be always looking and never finding, because eventually everyone is a disappointment. This emptiness is never filled. "Need love" says, "I love myself, and I want you."

The second kind of love, according to Lewis, is "gift love." Instead of an emptiness within which the lover seeks to fill with something seen in the loved one, there is something in the lover which he or she seeks to *give* to the loved one. The lover's greatest desire is simply to give. John Claypool, the minister, says that instead of being a circle such as "need love," which always goes out only to return to itself, "gift love" is an arc which goes out to stay with the loved person. Its one purpose is to give something out of itself to the person who is loved. This is God's kind of love.

In the beginning, God did not create the world because of some need he had. As someone put it, God found existence so wonderful, he wanted to share it. Creation was the act of God out of his fullness, his wanting to share. God had no desire to get anything for himself in the act of creation. The inference is made sometimes that humankind was created by God to love and serve God. In the truest sense, it would be much more accurate to say that God created humankind not so he would have someone to love and serve him, but so that he would have someone to love and to serve. And the greatest day in any person's life is the day that person accepts and is confident in this "gift love" of God.

This is what happened at the baptism of Jesus. We have what the theologians call anthropomorphism, which means giving to God the characteristics of human beings and having him speak out of heaven with a voice everyone understood, saying, "This is my beloved Son, in whom I take pleasure." But the most significant thing that happened at that baptism was that Jesus felt the full acceptance and approval of God. This is what sent him out to a life of service and ministry.

There is, in God's plan, acceptance of us by himself, and also his expectation of us. We have believed that the expectation comes before the acceptance, but it works just the other way. The acceptance comes *before* the expectation. We do not do good things to get God to love us. God loves us—therefore we do good things. This is the reason the story of the voice out of heaven, saying "This is my beloved Son in whom I take pleasure," came not at the end of Christ's ministry, on the cross, but at the beginning of his ministry, at the baptism. That statement of acceptance and pleasure by God came first, then came the life of service. And it is very significant that it did not take place in the reverse order. "Gift love" is simply that—it's a *gift*. It requires no measuring up; it does not ask that you compete or win; it does not wait for any deserving—it's a gift. And when you have the capacity to love this way, you have glory and beauty ever increasing in your life.

Now then, how does this apply to the lives you and I live personally—the different areas of our life?

First of all, *in the area of relationships between parents and children*. The greatest thing any parent can ever do for children is to love them with "gift love" rather than "need love."

Some of us as parents have a great need to live out our ambitions in our children. These personal ambitions seek to direct our children in their choice of friends, the school they attend, the job they take, and even the husbands or wives they marry. And in this process, we often give them the impression that they must earn our love and our approval. In fact, in certain situations, we may even sometimes say, "You must do so and so, or Mother won't love you" or "Daddy won't love you." Or sometimes we say, "I love you when you are good."

I have a preacher friend who says he never doubted his mother's love, but he always felt he had to continually earn it. She always said to him, "If you ever want to amount to anything, you must make something of yourself," and even though it was unspoken, he said, he felt that in order to hold her love and approval, he had to make something of himself.

When he went into the ministry, he said it was for several reasons, but at least one was that he thought it would please his mother. He said that he went to mail the letter telling her he had decided to go into the ministry, and after dropping the letter in the mailbox, he thought to himself, "Now she will love me, she will accept me, she will approve of me."

Only a miracle of conversion to the "gift love" of God could save my friend and enable him to love in this same way, because it is only after we experience "gift love" that we are enabled to live "gift love." And if our parents don't do it, then it takes a miracle of God to give us "gift love."

Our children must feel love and acceptance constantly, and always. We can disapprove of particular actions, but never disapprove of the children. We can say, "You cheated," but never say "You are a cheat." We can say, "That was an unwise thing you did," but never say, "You are stupid." We might say, "You lied about that," but never, "You are a liar." We can say, "You did not do your share in that project," but never, "You are lazy" or "You are no good." To be able to say, "My son never gave us a moment of concern," does not necessarily mean we were good parents. It is possible it means only that we loved him with a "need love." The need was not to worry about him, and the child met that need. It is possible that in the process the child was crippled for life in personality and the ability to be a whole person.

When I was in grade school, we used to have a spelling test on Friday evening. I don't know whether you had spelling on Friday afternoon or not. We had spelling words all week, and then we would have a test on Friday, and I don't know of anything more important to my mother than that I make a hundred in spelling on Friday. There were two of us who vied for making a hundred, and Mary Lois was the other one. If I went home with ninety-eight or ninety-nine or a hundred, the first question was, "What did Mary Lois make?" I just hated Mary Lois.

I never learned to spell. I made a hundred nearly every Friday, and I never learned to spell. On the last spelling test I took in college, I misspelled fifty-three words out of a hundred. The motive was wrong. My motive was to get that certain expression of approval from mother's face. "Gift love," which includes total acceptance with no requirement to earn it or to win it, is the greatest gift any parent gives a child.

Then the second area in which this is true is *in the relationship between husband and wife*. So often we married people keep trying to get our mates to change so we can love them properly. We have a need to love a certain person, and we insist that he or she meet that need.

For the first ten years of our marriage, I thought I was going to make my wife, Sue, over. I honestly thought that with enough effort on my part—a suggestion here, an innuendo there, a scolding at this point—I would finally get her to be the kind of person I needed her to become, the kind I could really love. Then one day I finally decided it wasn't working. In fact, the more I suggested, the plainer my innuendoes, the more severe my scolding, the worse she got. So I gave up, and I decided to love her as she was. And I discovered a wonderful person I had never known, because I was so busy trying to make her over.

"Gift love" is absolutely essential to a happy marriage. Without it, we would never find happiness, because sooner or later every person lets us down. "Need love" says, "I have a need, and I think you can fill it." "Gift love" says, "I have something to give, and I want to share it with you."

Finally, accepting *"gift love" in our relationship with God* is so very important.

The great Karl Barth—I suppose one of the greatest theologians of all time, certainly of modern times—came to Richmond, Virginia, to the Baptist Seminary to speak. After he had lectured, he went to the student union to visit with some of the students informally. They sat and talked, and finally one of them said to him, "Dr. Barth, you've written so much on theology, so many books, you've opened so many windows and doors to us in the world of theology. Could you sum it all up?"

And according to the story, Dr. Barth paused a long time, as European theologians are wont to do, and rubbed his face with his hands. Finally he lifted his face and said, "Yes, I can, I can sum it all up. 'Jesus loves me, this I know, for the Bible tells me so.' " Having written millions of words on theology, he could sum it all up in a simple children's song.

PRAYER

O Lord, our Heavenly Father, we go along through life so eager and so anxious and so busy, until we fail to examine the base from which we operate—the basic assumptions out of which we live and make our decisions. Father, help us occasionally to stop and search our deepest motives, especially in this particular area that is so very significant in human relations. Help us to put aside the demanding kind of love that seeks to fill our needs. Let us, in a miraculous way, become one of those few people who ever discover gift love—love that goes out with only one purpose: to share something within us with someone else. Thank you, Father, for the ability to love. Amen.

LOVE AND DISAGREE

When I was in the eighth grade, Miss Ethel moved to our community and went to work in Mrs. Brown's dress shop. Miss Ethel was the first divorced woman I ever saw—that is, to know I was looking at a divorced woman. No one ever knew the whole story about Miss Ethel, but from what bits and pieces I could gather from adult conversation when I was a child, I got the impression that Miss Ethel's husband was no good; that he had mistreated her and had done some very bad things, although I was never sure what they were; then he had left her.

Miss Ethel apparently moved to our town to get away from the memories and make a new beginning. As I look back over the years in retrospect, it may be that Miss Ethel was seeking to heal her own personal wounds by showing a beautiful and happy outward countenance, and by doing all the good she did in our community. But she became the saving ray of sunshine to a small group of young people in our home church.

She came into my life at exactly the right time. I

loved God; at times I even felt the personal presence of God; I wanted to be good, but church and church attendance seemed pretty dismal to me at times, and the community itself was not exciting to me. Then suddenly there was this beautiful, radiant person who had been through some mysterious tragedy but had risen above it all.

Even though she never said it in words, I remember having the very distinct feeling that God had helped her. Miss Ethel became our Sunday school teacher and the counselor of our youth group on Sunday night. And suddenly church, religion, God, and everything about it became very exciting. I could hardly wait to get to each meeting. She stayed with us all through high school, and that radiance never faded. She is one of the very few people in my life who never let me down, even for a moment, by temper or impatience.

By the time I was a senior in high school I had decided to become a minister, and Miss Ethel was one of the first people I told. On the night of our graduation (there were twenty-six in our class) the principal didn't hand out the diplomas alphabetically. I was the last one to get my diploma, and when I came down the steps dressed in my cap and gown and clutching that precious diploma in my hand, Miss Ethel was standing at the bottom of the steps, and she laid an imitation leather scrapbook in my hands. It was obviously a labor of love. She had clipped and carefully pasted into this book every choice bit of poetry and every famous quotation she had been able to gather in her entire lifetime, and she had written on the inside cover, "May this bless you as you live to bless others."

That fall I went away to college, and during the first visit back home, I discovered Miss Ethel was gone. I lost track of her; I never saw her again. But that scrapbook came to be a great inspiration in my life. For a good while the ideas for the sermons I preached came out of that scrapbook. It was before the days of photocopying, and I wish now I had a copy. But by the time the book finally fell apart, I had committed most of it to memory.

There were three favorite selections of mine in that scrapbook. The first is Ralph Cushman's poem "The Secret," and the scrapbook was my first introduction to it:

> I met God in the morning
>> When my day was at its best,
> And His presence came like sunrise,
>> Like a glory in my breast.
>
> All day long the Presence lingered,
>> All day long He stayed with me,
> And we sailed in perfect calmness
>> O'er a very troubled sea.
>
> Other ships were blown and battered,
>> Other ships were sore distressed,
> But the winds that seemed to drive them
>> Brought to us a peace and rest.
>
> Then I thought of other mornings,
>> With a keen remorse of mind,
> When I too had loosed the moorings,
>> With the Presence left behind.
>
> So I think I know the secret,
>> Learned from many a troubled way:

You must seek Him in the morning
If you want Him through the day!

The second of my favorite selections was "Myself,"
by Edgar Guest. It begins:

I have to live with myself, and so
I want to be fit for myself to know,
I want to be able, as days go by,
Always to look myself straight in the eye;
I don't want to stand, with the setting sun,
And hate myself for the things I've done.

I don't want to keep on a closet shelf,
A lot of secrets about myself,
And fool myself, as I come and go,
Into thinking that nobody else will know
The kind of a man that I really am;
I don't want to dress up myself in sham.

. . . .

Whatever happens, I want to be
Self-respecting and conscience free.

And then there was my third favorite, and that's
what I want to talk to you about. The third quotation
was printed on a small piece of yellow parchment
paper on a page by itself in the scrapbook, and this is
what it said: "One of the greatest lessons a person ever
learns is to disagree without becoming disagreeable."

Now, through the years I have become more and
more convinced that the cause of most human
unhappiness in the world, all the way from the most
personal problems to those historic conflicts throughout the world, is that people just don't know how to

disagree without becoming disagreeable. I think this quotation has meant so much in my life because I was later than most people in learning that a person can differ with me and still love me. One can disapprove of something about me or something I do, and still love me. It took me a long time to understand that people who love us most are usually the most likely to differ with us openly and to our faces. In fact, often when those who sometimes express disapproval most personally to us—it is a symbol that they love us. The people who don't love us don't disagree with us to our faces. They avoid us and talk about us to others.

Now of course, "mother love" is the perfect example of love from our severest critics, being those who love us most. For most of us, no one in our lives can speak more critically, try harder to mold us and change us, and disapprove of something we have done more severely than a mother; and still in the midst of her disapproval of our habits or our actions, there is no one of whose love we are more certain. This kind of mother love is the best example of the ability to love and disagree. Now the big question, of course, is: How does this apply to your daily life, and to mine?

I would like to deal with this in two parts. First, how do we differ lovingly and without becoming disagreeable? And second, how do we accept differences expressed by others without feeling unloved, and becoming disagreeable?

First of all, *we can differ without becoming disagreeable simply by being sensitive to the way we differ.* A tremendous amount of hurt and alienation takes place not because of differences, but simply because of the way those differences are expressed.

I'm sure you have known people who can express a very minor difference in such a way that it becomes a major issue. A few years ago, right after Interstate 20 was completed through Shreveport, my wife, Sue, and I made a trip to Dallas with another couple. The other husband was driving, and as we approached one exit on the highway just about a third of the way there, he slowed down and said, "Let's stop at this little place and get a cup of coffee."

His wife said, "No, not at this greasy-spoon place. You always pick out the most unsavory places to eat." Then he drove on without a word.

She turned around to us in the back seat and said, "I don't know why, but he has absolutely no taste when it comes to choosing places to eat or to stay. You wouldn't believe some places we've stayed and eaten through the years." And then she said, "But, of course, I ought to understand, his father was just like him." And on and on she went until she had covered every possible lack of taste in him or his family. I felt sorry for him—all he had done was say, "Let's stop and get a cup of coffee."

The question of where to stop was not the point. It was how her difference was expressed. How easy it would have been for her to say, "That sounds good. I'd like a cup of coffee, but that place doesn't look too comfortable. Why don't we look for a place where we can rest a while and enjoy our coffee."

One of the classic examples I have ever seen of mastering the art of differing and saying it exactly right was given by a young woman of twenty-three who wanted to marry a young man her parents very much disapproved of. (Now, of course, when they objected to him so strongly, she *should* have considered their reasons for disapproval.) But she decided to marry him anyway.

She called them into the living room one evening, got them seated, and then she said, "I've been wanting to talk with you and tell you how much I love you, how much I appreciate everything you have done. I love you more than anyone, and I have all my life. I wouldn't hurt you for anything. I have looked forward to my marriage being a joy for you. I want your blessings, but you have taught me through the years that I must do what I believe is right, and I believe it's right for me to marry Jim. I want more than anything for you to love him as I do. I want your blessings, but I feel I must tell you I'm going to marry Jim."

Now this is expressing a *big* difference in a beautiful way. The first way to differ without becoming disagreeable is to be sensitive to the way we express our differences.

Second, *we can differ without becoming disagreeable if we are sensitive to how we have sufficiently expressed our differences.* May I repeat that? We can differ without becoming disagreeable if we are sensitive to how we have sufficiently expressed our differences. One of the greatest causes of strife is the repeated expression of the same differences over and over again—for years sometimes—until the issue ceases to be what it was in the beginning and only becomes an expression of stubbornness or hostility or nagging. After we have expressed a difference in the right way, and sufficiently to be clearly understood, then we should be extremely careful about continuing to express it.

Recently I was talking to a woman who said she had come to the end of her rope about certain things her husband did. She said, "I have tried every way, everything. What can I do now?" I said, "Just love him and pray for him." She said, "And let him go on like he's going?" And I said, "Now I'm sure you have told him exactly how you feel on several occasions." She said, "Every day for twenty years." I said, "Then he knows how you feel, and telling him again is not going to help. He doesn't hear you anymore." If you and I have a difference with someone—especially someone we are close to—which we have often expressed, it is very likely that from now on, every time we express it, we are not doing good, but harm.

Finally, *we can disagree without becoming disagreeable if we continue to love and to trust, in the midst of and in spite of that difference.* The truth is that all kinds of expressions of differences cannot accomplish some things that just quiet loving can accomplish. Saying these things over and over again cannot accomplish what patient love and trust can.

One of the great saints of all time was Saint Augustine. He lived during the latter part of the fourth and early part of the fifth century. He was born in North Africa. He was such a brilliant boy that his parents saw that he got every possible educational advantage. But when he was in his late teens, he morally rebelled against every family principle.

He broke his mother's heart; she pleaded with him to change, but to no avail. Over and over she expressed her disappointment and concern at the life he was living. She told him of her disappointment and concern repeatedly, and the crowning blow came when he told her one day that he was going to leave their home in North Africa and move to Milan, Italy, the most wicked city of the day. It had a terrible reputation. She was greatly concerned and feared her son would be destroyed morally.

But for some reason she was able, when she found that he was going in spite of everything she could do, to give him her blessing and tell him she loved him and trusted him. In her letters she never gave him any words of advice.

Then to her amazement, it was in Milan that he came under the influence of Saint Ambrose, the Bishop of Milan, and was converted to Christianity. Augustine then became one of the most influential Christian leaders and theologians of all history. His mother had thought his move to Milan was the last straw, the symbol of hopelessness. But she decided simply to love him and trust him, and it became the beginning of the healing of all their differences. There comes a time when we have expressed our differences enough, and we ought to love and to trust.

Those were suggestions as to how we can disagree without becoming disagreeable. Now, just a word about how we can *accept* disagreement without feeling unloved and becoming disagreeable.

The main point to remember is that when people disagree with us, it does not mean they don't love us. It often means they do. I learned a long time ago, and I wish I had learned much earlier, that often the people who differ with me most in the church, and who express it most openly, are the ones who love me the most. Those who do not love us seldom disagree with us in person.

There is a dear lady in our church who, years ago, I used to be afraid to meet because she always had a suggestion about something I ought to do better. Then one day it dawned on me—she loved me so much that, as she traveled throughout the community, she couldn't stand to hear anybody say any critical word about me. She wanted to fix it, she wanted me to be perfect because she loved me. We ought to remember that when persons differ with us, it's usually a symbol that they are the ones who love us.

Now then, it must be said, with all these suggestions about how to disagree without being disagreeable or to accept disagreement without feeling rejected, that it is not possible to do this without a basic change of spirit in the person. You don't just make up your mind to do this. Most of us have made up our minds to do differently about many things so many times, and we do not have the strength and the power to do it.

This is the reason we here are known as an evangelical church. We believe a person has to be converted in the inner spirit of the soul, in a basic and major rebirth, in order to be able to do these things.

You and I have made our resolutions over and over. We intend to do better. We hope to respond differently, but under pressure when we don't have time to think, that basic nature comes out, and we do the same old thing the same old way.

It takes a basic surrender and commitment. It takes an evangelical experience of the love of God to change us in our basic nature, because in most circumstances we don't have time to think about being nice and good and loving. In most significant moments of life, we react out of what we are inside, rather than acting analytically and logically, and so it takes a basic spiritual experience to change our very natures in order to do this. This is what Paul was talking about in that beautiful thirteenth chapter of First Corinthians on love. Read it again, for it describes the kind of love that none of us is capable of, without the help of God.

PRAYER

Father, on this wonderful day our hearts are full of love and appreciation. It is true that most of us have our highest and lowest moments in our family relationships. This is where we are capable of the greatest joy and greatest sorrow. We can take what happens to us outside; we can survive our professional disappointments; we can handle differences with friends and neighbors—it is at home where it gets us! If we can make it all right at home, we can take anything else outside. And so it's today that we especially turn our attention to being able to love and differ with those we love and differ with the most. Help us to make this wonderful and great discovery today; in Jesus' name. Amen.

HOW TO MAKE LOVE

W hat is the first thing you think about when you
hear the words *make love?* What is the first
thing that comes to your mind?

I was coming home on a plane from a preaching
engagement one night recently, and I happened to be
sitting by a young woman who was reading a
paperback book. I couldn't help noticing that on
almost every page, and sometimes several times on
the page, there were two words in bold italic type. The
two words were *made love.* It apparently was the story
of the interrelationships of several people in a very
sophisticated modern circumstance, and apparently
they made love here and there and just about
everywhere.

Since this sermon subject has been on my mind for
some time, I very much wanted to ask that young lady
what she thought the phrase meant, but I was afraid
she would have me arrested or would have thought
something very bad about me. Even if she hadn't had
me arrested or thought I was an evil person, she most
certainly would have looked at my gray hair and my

bald head and my obvious age and wondered, "Where in the world have you been all these years?"

Of course, I did not ask her—I did not need to ask her. It's almost certain that she thought it meant what the writer had very likely meant for her to think it meant, and what so much of our society, so many movies, television shows, and novels have taught her.

Probably the very worst thing that has happened in our American culture, and in fact the whole modern culture, is that this all-encompassing word *love*—which originally designated the creative force which brought everything into existence—has been narrowed in its meaning to be thought of almost exclusively in terms of one very limited aspect of the vast part it plays in human life and all creation. This one aspect of love, which comes to the mind of almost every modern person in American society when the word love is mentioned, is romantic love.

And when the words *make love* or *made love* are used, the meaning narrows even more and becomes one specific physical experience between a man and a woman, at a particular time and in a particular place.

In the little book *The Key to Power in Personal Life*, written in 1954 and later issued under the title *Three Magic Words*, W. S. Anderson says this in a graphic way. Here's what he wrote:

> Much has been written and said about love, poets have extolled it and musicians have sung about it, ballads and plays and stories are ever unfolding its many-sided drama. Here is the truth about love, they say, and then they present romantic love, a partial truth only, and nearly all the world is deluded. This surging, welling inspirational searching that throbs

within the breast of every human being, this thing called love, can never be reduced only to rapport between the sexes.

Our literature and our education have inhibited us until we believe that the end-all of love is finding a mate and mating. Our divorce courts and our psychiatrists' offices are literally filled with multitudes of unhappy and disillusioned people who have discovered that this just is not so. If there is one thing a vast number of human experiences in marriage and various kinds of mating have taught us in recent years, it is that what we have generally chosen to accept as "making love" does not in fact make love at all. As important as this part of human life may be in its right perspective, this is not the way you make love in the truest sense. In fact, when out of its proper perspective, it can be a serious and tragic block to making love in the most satisfying and lasting permanent sense.

Now of course, if this very commonly accepted interpretation of how to make love is not true, then how *do* you do it? How do you go about making love in your own life and in the lives of others very close to you and in the world in which we live? Let me make a few suggestions.

First, *if we are going to make love, it must be universal and all-inclusive.* We cannot love one person properly until we love all people. No person can love another person properly until he or she loves humanity first. Real, satisfying, lasting, fulfilling love can never be selective. We can't say, "I will love this person, but I will not love that one." Each time we refuse to love anyone it makes us less able to love any other one. If we are going to make love a reality in our lives and in the lives of others, it must be universal. We must love everyone.

This takes place, of course, by realizing and recognizing the basic truth of the unity of all life. Once I have realized this completely—that I and my neighbor are one—it is no longer possible for me to do anything to hurt him or her. It would be the same as doing it to myself. Nor can I hate even my enemy, for my enemy is also one with me, as much a part of myself as I am. The famous and often repeated words of John Donne—in his poem formerly titled "Meditation 13," more commonly known as "For Whom the Bell Tolls"—express this truth more graphically than any other in the English language.

Before I quote Donne, let me explain to young people, who may not have had an opportunity to know, what it means to toll a bell. In Europe and in the early days of America, and in fact in my own hometown when I was a young boy, the church bell was the emergency alarm and the news agency of the community. If there was a fire in the middle of the night the bell would ring violently and rapidly, alerting everyone to get dressed and hurry to help save a neighbor's home. If there was good news, the bell would ring moderately and sweetly, giving out a happy sound, announcing that a war was over or a baby was born or a wedding had taken place.

Then there was a special sound of the bell when someone died. It was called "tolling the bell." I've done it many times myself. You pull the rope on the big bell just enough until the clapper inside of it hits just one side of the bell but not the other, and when you do this the bell will take on a mournful sound . . . dong . . . dong . . . dong. And you know that somebody has died.

John Donne, in his poem "For Whom the Bell Tolls," says, "No man is an island. Each is a part of the whole. Just as each clod of earth that falls into the sea diminishes England, each man's death diminishes me. And therefore, never send to know for whom the bell tolls. It tolls for thee."

Jesus said we are to love all people as if they are part of ourselves. Literally, he said, "Love your neighbor as yourself." I cannot hate a person of another race; I cannot hate capital or labor or the Russians or the Ayatollah Khomeini or anyone else without, to some extent, losing my ability to properly love my wife, or my son, or my little granddaughters, or you. My lack of love for even my worst enemy steals a little of the richness and the sweetness out of my love for the ones I do choose to love.

We even feel sometimes that we can get people to love us more if we get them to love someone else less. We go so far as to try to get them to dislike some other person. The result is that we are only robbing ourselves by seeking to take from others their love.

Of course it goes without saying that there are different kinds of love. There's love of husband or wife, there's love of sister or brother, there's love for parents or for grandparents or for friends or an associate, there is love for the passing stranger, and there's love for our enemies. They are all different and express themselves in different ways. But however it is expressed, the word in its broadest sense means "active good will." And even though the emotions may be different, love is willing good for all people, and the willingness to give ourselves for their welfare. If we are to *make love*, it must be universal and all inclusive.

Second, *love must include every aspect of life*. It not only must include everyone, it must include every part of life—not just one part. To try to limit love to one part of life, such as the physical experience with a mate, is to eventually destroy even that part of love which we search for so eagerly. We can't love in one part of life or one activity of life without loving in all its parts. We can't cheat a person in a business deal or be unkind to a clerk or a waitress or a hired hand; we can't be selfish in any part of life without its taking something out of a love relationship in which we do honestly want to give ourselves unselfishly to some other person. If I live a lie in any part of my life, it takes from the ring of truth in every other part of life, and in everything I do.

One time I went to speak at a lecture series at a church in another state. Sue was with me, and we were to be there four nights. After the first meeting, the pastor took us to a motel—or at least it was called a motel. It was the original tourist court that was ever built! There were cabins with little lean-tos for garages and they had screen doors with a spring on them. Our cabin had a bed that felt like a hammock.

Sue just rolled right down on top of me when we got in bed, and I said to her, "If I try to sleep in this bed, I can't preach this week."

She said, "You know the pastor said that this motel belonged to a member of the church board."

I said, "Yes, I know that, but if I have to sleep in this bed, I can't preach." Then I said, "Do you remember that new Holiday Inn about eighteen or twenty miles back?"

She said "Yes."

I said "Let's go up there."

So we got up, and we messed up the bed real good and put some towels on the floor in the bathroom; then we went out and got in the car and very quietly started it. We didn't turn on the lights until we were outside on the highway, and we drove back and registered in the Holiday Inn.

Every night we went through that ritual. We would go over and mess up the bed and put towels on the floor. It just worried me to death! I'd get up to preach and all I could see were those two hotel rooms. I wouldn't have felt any worse if I were having an affair with somebody on the side.

We made it through the last night. We thought we had tricked everybody. When anybody would ask if we were comfortable, we would say "Yes, we are very comfortable."

The last night I sat down in the pulpit, and while we were singing a hymn and I was getting ready to preach the last sermon, a man came in and handed something to the pastor, and he came over and handed me a key. He said, "You turned in the wrong key at the hotel where we had you registered."

In my excitement, I had turned in the Holiday Inn key to the man on the board of the church!

As we drove home, I told Sue, "I don't care if they put us in a tent from now on, I'm going to stay there."

If you're living a lie in any part of your life, it touches every other part. We can't segregate parts of our lives. It is one of the major errors of our time to think of making love primarily in a certain area of life, or as a certain activity of life. A satisfactory physical experience of sex is the result of love, not the cause of it. People who seek sexual love exclusively, or even primarily, never find it. They may try more and more desperately, only to find less and less satisfaction. Real fulfillment in this area of life is a *by-product*. The sexual relationship, no matter how we may feel at the moment, does not make love. If it's real, love *makes it*. The satisfactory act of sex is not making love; it is rather one of the many results of *having made love* in every part of life.

Third, *love must include all circumstances and all situations*. We cannot love under certain circumstances and not under others, and when we try, we cease to truly love under *any* circumstances. If I determine that I will love under certain circumstances but I will not love under others, then I determine my ability to truly love at all, even under the best circumstances in which I choose to do my loving. If I decide that my wife could do enough things to displease me that I would stop loving her, then I am less able to love her properly even when she is doing everything to please me.

Our love for everyone in all aspects of life must be unconditional—that is, everyone in all parts of life, under all conditions. This is the way you make love.

The single greatest tragedy of our time is lack of ability to make an unconditional commitment to anything or anyone. Total life commitment is one thing that has almost disappeared from serious thinking in our personal lives today. But thank God there is a little light on the horizon that seems to indicate it's turning around.

Some months ago I heard a new story. I thought I'd heard them all. A young girl came to be married; she was eighteen years old, the boy was nineteen. When they are that age, I always say, "What do your folks think about this?"

So I said, "What does your mother think about your marriage?"

She answered, "She disapproves."

I said, "Does she not like this boy?"

She replied, "Oh no, she likes him. She disapproves of *marriage*. Mother said, 'Why don't you live with him? Why clutter your life with marriage?' "

The mother had been married and divorced three times. She was a "child of the sixties" when they wanted to write their own vows, take none of the traditional ones, sing to guitar music, and be married in the yard barefooted.

This young lady wanted all the traditional vows. She wanted someone to sing, "I Love You Truly." And one phrase she said a half-a-dozen times: "Don't leave anything out. I don't want to be like my mother." Thank God there seems to be some return to life commitment.

There are two kinds of love. One says plainly, "I love you. I give myself to you." The other says, "I love myself and I want you; I need you; you please me. I like what you can do for *me*." This second kind is always temporary. There will come a time when you displease me and I won't want you.

Young people, when they say to you, "I want you; I need you; I can't live without you," it may sound good, but if it's true, you better look out. If the main thing they are feeling is a need for you and what you can do for them, the seeds of destruction are already sown. Their paramount thought must be what they can do for *you*, and the same thing must be true in *your* heart, or you'd better not marry.

Finally, *if we are to make love, we must include God*. It must be infinite in nature. The Scripture says we love one another because he has first loved us. We must realize and know, as a personal experience, the love of God, the forgiveness of God. God accepts us as we are under any condition and, as the Scripture says, "died for us while we were yet sinners." When we didn't deserve anything, he loved us. Until we have accepted that—and cast our lot with that and adopted that—then we cannot truly love any person.

A person doesn't learn to love by being taught to do so. A person learns to love by being loved, and no one can do that like God can do it. In the best of human love there are little weak spots, and we keep working on those weak spots, but in the love of God there are no weak spots. He doesn't have to work at it. God *is* love. When we adopt that—and accept that—and cast our lives with that, then we are enabled to love.

Many a person who is having trouble in love relationships goes to a psychologist or a psychiatrist who, in many instances when people are mentally ill, can do a lot of good; but very often you keep going; the doctor keeps working, picking out this little thing and that little thing that keeps you from loving. This goes on for months and years, picking up little things that made you like you are, and it works.

But there's something else that works also, and that's total conversion in the *grace* of God; this is what the Scripture calls being born again, as if there were no experiences before. They are all wiped out at one time, and that ability to love properly is given to us—not by digging every little experience out of the past, but by forgetting the past. That is what the good news of the gospel is—God loves us in the way we can love everybody else. This, I believe, is how you *make love*.

PRAYER

Heavenly Father, it is true of us all. We all want to be loved and, equally, we all want to love. We not only just want to be loved, we want to love. But for so many of us, something stands in the way. We find ourselves unable to love and give ourselves totally and completely in trust to anyone, making ourselves open and available to be hurt or even destroyed; we just can't bring ourselves to do it. And we find that we doubt even what seems to be the most sincere expression of love. We begin to try to pick it apart and wonder if it's true. We doubt our own ability and the ability of others to love. Father, if there is anything we need in our society and in the lives we live today, it's to understand the meaning of love. We ask for that understanding to begin today anew. In the name of the One who loved us so much that, while we were yet sinners, he died for us, even Jesus. Amen.

SOME TESTS FOR TRUE LOVE

*T*here is a passage from the third chapter of First John which says, "We know that we have passed from death unto life, because we love."

Throughout the Bible we have the assurance that this passage is true, that the real test of the Christian life is love. The thing that has bothered me is the fact that we do not know whether or not we love. One of the great difficulties with so many people who have spiritual difficulty and problems in life is the fact that they do not *realize* they do not love.

So often we have never discovered the ability to love, and we do not *know* we have not discovered that ability. Very often we attribute our great difficulties to some other cause, when actually the reason is our inability to love.

It's true that the real test of passing from death unto life is the ability to love, but what is the real test of true love? How do we *know* when we love? It is certainly true that many who say they love, do not. Everything that goes under the name of love is not really love.

Some time ago there was an article in a newspaper

about a man who had shot and killed his ailing wife. When he was questioned, he said over and over, "I loved her too much to see what was happening to her."

I know of a mother who deliberately broke up her daughter's marriage and brought her back to her own home. She broke up that home with deceit and suggestions, many of them untrue.

I said to her, "This is what you did, isn't it?"

Finally she said, "Yes."

Then I said, "Why did you do this?"

And she said, "I loved her so much—I loved her too much to see her leave home."

It's obvious that everything that goes under the name of love is not love, but something entirely different. Whatever it is, it's not love. One of the great problems of life is to know what love is, and what the test of true love is, and whether or not we possess that true love.

We often assume that there are only two problems in love. The first is that we believe we must be attractive enough to be loved. The second major problem, we think, is finding somebody to love. We assume that these are our two major problems with love, but they are not.

The major problem in love is the *ability* to love. It's not just being attractive ourselves, or finding the proper object for our love. The chief problem is our own inner ability to love—that is, whether we are capable of true love.

Take, for instance, the idea that we must be attractive, that one of our main problems is to make ourselves lovable. This is a very popular notion today.

People feel that if they want to be loved, they must make themselves attractive. I read the advice to the lovelorn columns in the newspapers occasionally, and the other day a lady wrote that she was losing her husband, that he was interested in somebody else. "What can I do?" she said.

The "expert" told her to go on a diet, exercise, and get a new hair cut, then described all the ways the woman could recapture her husband's love.

We have never learned that only love, not just attractiveness, produces love. Some of the most attractive people you ever meet are not loved. It isn't attractiveness that produces love. Our own ability to love produces love. If people would be loved, their time should be spent not only making themselves attractive, but time also should be spent developing their ability to love.

Then the other mistaken idea is that the "object" of love is the important thing. We assume that it is easy to love, that the important and difficult thing is to find the *right person* to love. Of course this is not true.

A few weeks ago a woman said to me, "I don't love him anymore." She was planning to get a divorce.

I said, "Why don't you love him?"

She said, "Well, I just don't love him anymore." She was assuming that the problem was in the *object* of her love, when her real problem was *her inability* to love. It was as obvious as it could be. She will continue to break up her home because she no longer loves that particular object of her love. She is assuming that this is the problem, when it is not in the least.

Now, what *are* the tests of true love? Here are some. Maybe they will suggest some others to you.

The first test of true love is *care*. "Mother love" is often used as the classic example of true love. What makes it the classic example? It is *caring*.

Anyone who professes to love, but does not show care, does not really love. It makes no difference how much a mother professes to love a child, if she neglects the care of that child—neglects to bathe it, feed it properly, make it physically comfortable—that mother does not truly love.

Any person who professes to love but does not show great care and concern has missed the point. That is not true love.

Some years ago a woman came to my office with a little girl. She came for counseling. The mother had great problems. When she came for counseling she had no place to leave the little girl, so she brought her along. When they came in she sat the little girl over on the chair across from us. The mother was beautifully groomed, but the little girl's hair was stringy and dirty. She apparently had not had her little shoes cleaned in weeks.

I knew what the woman's problem was before she ever opened her mouth—the *inability to love*. Anyone who does not *care*, does not have tender care, does not love. Show me some children and their house, and I can tell whether their parents have the ability to love.

Even with animals and plants, this is true. If people say, "I love flowers," but forget to water them, you don't think much of their love for flowers. They let them die on the windowsill because they forget to water them.

Care is one of the most powerful evidences of love. Eric Fromm, the wonderful philosopher of our day and age, says, "Love is the active concern for the life and growth of that which we love. Where active concern is lacking, there is no love."

I went to a home the other day where a woman was very unhappy. She said her husband didn't love their home as much as she did, and he didn't want to come home. He ought to love the home the way she loved it. But at one o'clock in the afternoon, the house looked as if she had just gotten up. The breakfast and lunch dishes were in the sink and the beds were unmade. No matter how much she professed to love her home, she was registering every day her lack of love. She wanted her husband home for selfish reasons, not because she wanted him to love it like she loved it, and he knew that. Care is a true test of love.

Young people who do not show care for their mothers and fathers do not love their mothers and fathers properly. The teenage girl who speaks sharply to her father, the teenage boy who lets his mother mow the yard, trim the grass, and pick up sticks under the trees may *say* he loves his mother, and he may cry so you can hear him all over the funeral home when his mother dies, but he does not *truly* love his mother. We can't love without *care*.

The second test I would like to mention is *responsibility*. I was reading again the other day an account of the beginnings of the human race, and I ran across the idea that Adam didn't really love Eve. I had never thought about whether Adam loved Eve or not. This was the statement: "Adam did not love Eve because he would not take responsibility for Eve. He not only would not take responsibility for Eve, but he put his responsibility on her, and therefore he could not have loved her."

The willingness to accept responsibility is a true test for love. If you really love someone, you are willing to take responsibility for that person.

Every now and then a couple comes to the counseling room, and they will spend an hour talking—each one saying the other one is totally to blame for their bad relationship. When they do so, they are not telling anyone about each other—they are telling about themselves, their own inability to love properly.

It's a beautiful thing to see a person who stays true and who protects and gives excuses for the other person. Even though the world may know that those excuses are not real, it's a beautiful thing. I love to see a wife and a husband, even though they have little ground to stand on, defend the one they love and take responsibility for each other.

This is the thing that is perfectly portrayed in Jesus upon the cross. He was taking responsibility for all of us. This is the thing that down through history has been the conclusive proof of how he loved us. Taking *responsibility* for someone is a test of true love. I know a man who professes to love his family, but when he gets his paycheck he puts it in a personal account of his own. He doles out to his wife what he feels she should use and doles out money to his children. Time and time again, he refuses flatly to take responsibility when they are in difficulty, causing embarrassment to both his wife and his children. That man does not love. A man who truly loves takes responsibility for his family and his home.

Some time ago a man sat in my office and complained about his wife's hospital bills. He complained that her family hadn't paid any of her hospital bills. If that man loved as he should, he would work twenty-four hours a day for the privilege of paying every dollar of the hospital bills of the one he loved.

Responsibility is a test of love. If you find yourself quick to accept responsibility for others, then you have true love. If you and I find ourselves quick to blame other people, we had better check up on our love.

The third test for love is *respect*. The word *respect* comes from a Latin word that means to look at, or to see something as it really is. To respect persons is to see them as they really are and to love them as they are, not as we would like for them to be or need them to be. Love them as they are.

The other day a girl said to me about the boy she is going to marry, "Well, he isn't exactly what I wanted *either* [her mother was objecting], but I'm going to change him." In the first place, she has an impossible task. In the second place, she doesn't really love him. When you love, you love people as they are. If we are still trying to make them over as we'd like to see them, then we don't really love. We must love them as they are.

If I love you, I love you as you are. The old invitation hymn we used to sing says, "Just as I am, without one plea, but that Thy blood was shed for me, I come." The wonderful good news is that God loves us as we are. "While we were yet sinners Christ died for us," the Scripture says.

True love loves as a person is, not as we would like for him or her to be. If we are capable of true love, we always love people not for what they are, but *in spite* of what they are.

The last test of love is *knowledge of the person.* You have often heard it said, "To know him is to love him," and that's true of all people. To know them is to love them. The sad thing is that so many of us go through life living with people and never knowing them. For many of us, the great tragedy of our lives is that we never really know any other human being. When you know persons only on the surface, you may see that they have a temper, or that they lie occasionally, or that they stretch the truth. But when you really get to know them, you see *why* they have a temper and the *reason* they stretch the truth, and then you love them.

If you truly love, you love people in spite of their weaknesses, because you know them and understand them. It makes no difference what your child and mine do, we love them. We see their weaknesses, but we know *why* they do the things they do because we know them, and so we continue to be loving, forgiving, and understanding.

Of course, the only way to know anybody else and to love anybody else, the Scripture tells us, is to know God and to love God, because God is love. Suddenly, when you know God, you can know other people.

I was talking to a man the other day after he had been converted and had gone back home and lived for a while. He said, "You know, I never knew how wonderful the people in my family are. I never knew them. I've been living with them all these years, and I never really knew them. I live with some wonderful people."

When you know God, you get to *know* people, and you discover true love. "We know that we have passed from death unto life, because we love," and "My little children, love not in word or in tongue, but in deed and in truth."

PRAYER

O Lord, our Heavenly Father, one of our great difficulties is that we do not realize that we do not love. We wonder if we are going to be held accountable, Father, for the fact that we didn't know. Is it possible that we can go through life not even knowing that we don't love, and then find death at the end of the way? Is it possible that the only way to pass from death unto life is to love properly? How is it, Father, that we go from year to year, never really loving anybody, and not knowing that we don't love anybody? Heavenly Father, if it is true that this is the only way to pass from death unto life, there must be a way for all of us to understand. It wouldn't be fair. There must be a way that we can all know whether or not we love. Help us to look for it and to test our love, to be honest about it, because it must be a matter of life and death that we love properly. Bless us with this great blessing; in Jesus' name, Amen.

LOVE ME—LOVE WHAT I DO

O ne of the most difficult things Jesus had to do while he was upon the earth was to convince his followers that he had come to save them *in* their present situation, not *out* of it. If by saving them *in* their situation, it happened as a result to bring them *out* of their situation, then this was a by-product, but not the original purpose of his mission. Still the most difficult thing for many of us who claim to be his followers to believe and accept, is that he is our Savior because he gives heavenly quality to life *now . . . here.* He saves us *in* this life, not primarily *out* of this life.

I spend quite a bit of my time driving alone in an automobile, and when I get in, usually I turn on the cassette player I have in the car. It reads a monthly condensation of several major magazines and periodicals to me. There are articles on it of a religious nature or related to religion, such as philosophy, psychology, ethics or sociology, as well as several other related fields. This is a wonderful thing to have, because in a few hours you can get what it would take hundreds of hours to read on your own.

But sometimes the tapes for the month have run out, and I will turn the radio on to one of the religious broadcast stations. When I do, I'm constantly amazed at what passes for religion, especially some of what passes for the Christian religion. If people out there, those who do not really know, get the impression that *this* is what the Christian faith is all about, I don't blame them if they don't want to have anything to do with it.

One evening some time ago I was driving back into the city after being out on a speaking engagement; I was driving along, listening to one of the all-religious stereo stations, and a man and a woman were singing with beautiful orchestral accompaniment. They were singing as if they were in heaven, and they sang these words: "We've enjoyed ten million years and our joy has only just begun." Then the song went on: "The battle's over." It sounded very warm and beautiful and triumphant.

But the main message of the Christian gospel is to save us in the *midst* of the battle, not *out* of the battle. In fact, it is entirely possible that the battle will not be over and that we had better learn to enjoy it and be saved in it. There is very good evidence that this is the best of all worlds God could create, giving us free will, and unless God is going to take away that free will, then the next world will be an opportunity only for a greater struggle at a higher level in our search for truth.

If you and I are waiting to be saved *out* of the struggle, then we have missed the point of what Jesus called victory in this life. Jesus said that when we pray we should say, "Our Father which art in Heaven,

Hallowed be thy name. Thy kingdom come. Thy will be done *in earth*, as it is in heaven." And he also said, "I came that you might have life, and have it more abundantly," and apparently he meant have it *here* and *now*.

This is in line with such of Jesus' statements as "the kingdom of heaven is within you," and also in line with that famous exchange he had with Thomas and Phillip. You remember. Thomas said, "Lord, we know not whither thou goest, how *can* we know the way?" Jesus answered, "Thomas, *I am* the way. No man comes to the Father but by me."

Then Phillip said, "Lord, show us the Father, and we will be satisfied." And Jesus gave this very interesting answer to Phillip. He said, "Have I been so long with you, Phillip, and yet you have not known me? If you have seen me, you have seen the Father. The Father and I are one."

In other words, Jesus is saying to Phillip and Thomas and the rest of the disciples, "Why do you keep waiting for something? It's all available to you already, here and now." Jesus obviously taught that it is possible to have that heavenly quality in this life, and what is even better, he gave specific instructions as to how we can accomplish it.

Probably the most important of those instructions was that we must learn to love people, even when we cannot love everything they do; and we must learn to accept the love of other people, who do not always love everything *we* do. This was the first step in the discovery of this kingdom of heaven upon earth.

Now, of course, the perfect example of this is given on the cross when he looked down at those crucifying him and said, "Father, forgive them for they know not what they do." He loved them even though what they were doing was taking his life. He loved them even when he could not love what they were doing, and he loved them enough to give his life for them.

Now the big question is, *How* do we do this? How do we get this kingdom of heaven within us now, when the strong tendency on the part of so many of us is to insist that if you love me, you must love everything I do, and if you don't love everything I do, then you don't love me? Here are some suggestions:

First of all, *we should remember the simple fact that people's tastes and preferences differ.* Often these differences in taste and preference have nothing to do with whether or not they love us.

In one of our first churches, there was a woman who had, for many years, been a soloist in the choir. From all accounts she was a very good one, but she was an elderly lady, and it was evident to everyone except herself that the time for soloing had passed.

We hired a young choir director who was just beginning in his profession, and I'm sure he heard several times from people, "Don't ask Mrs. So-and-So to sing a solo," and sure enough, she sang less and less.

Then one day when he and I were coming out of the church office, she met us right in the door. She was a large, outspoken woman, and she stood squarely in front of him and said, "Why don't you like me? What have I done to make you not like me?"

Maybe it was because he was young or because he believed in coming straight to the point, but he said, "I do like you, I just don't like to hear you sing." Then, as if this were not enough, he said, "There are a lot of people who like you that don't like to hear you sing."

Then suddenly she turned to me and she said, "Doctor Dykes, you like to hear me sing, don't you?" The whole thing had taken me so by surprise, I said, "I like nearly everything you do."

Looking back, I realize that the young choir director was so right. A lot of people did like her but did not like to hear her sing. And her insistence that if they loved her they must love everything she did, could have destroyed her.

But by a miracle with which God protects the young and the innocent, I suppose, she apparently took to heart what the young choir director said. She gracefully retired from singing solos. She became his greatest supporter and his assistant choir director.

Then something very difficult to believe happened later. On several occasions, she was asked to perform solos for other groups in the church. And by careful selection and the choir director's assistance, she showed she still had a remarkable voice in certain ranges, and she was greatly appreciated. I think it released a beauty within her, when she didn't have to make everybody like everything she did if they were to love her.

Many a young wife has destroyed peace in her home because she insisted that if her husband did not like everything she cooked, he did not love her. Many a young husband has caused great heartache by insisting that if his wife loved him, she would always do everything his way. We could save ourselves a great deal of trouble if we could just remember that people have differing tastes and preferences, and most of the time, it has nothing to do with whether they love us or not.

Then also, *we must remember that often our most treasured relationships are with people who know more of our faults than anyone else, and they still love us.* Our best friends are not those who always agree with us and approve of everything we do. Our best friends, whether within the family circle or outside of it, are those who will tell us our faults and love us at the same time.

I'm thinking of a woman who destroyed the people she loved best, especially her children. She made them feel they had to be perfect. She could not admit anything was ever wrong with someone she loved. This, of course, came across to them as saying, "Mother cannot love us if we are not perfect." Knowing they were not perfect, they subconsciously came to the conclusion that Mother does not love us. It would have been so much better if she could have admitted and faced their faults and loved them at the same time.

Recently I received an anonymous letter, and anonymous letters are always interesting to me. Every time I get one, I can't help but think of the story about Phillips Brooks, that famous Boston minister of the last generation. On one occasion he received a letter, and when he opened and unfolded it, there was just one word printed in large letters—FOOL.

The next Sunday morning when he stood up to preach, he told about the letter, and he said, "I have often received letters where the writer has written the letter and forgotten to sign a name; this is the first time

I have ever received one where the writer signed his name and forgot to write the letter."

This was not true of the letter I received. This anonymous letter was not an attack on me; it was an attack on someone else and written to me, which, of course, is worse. The writer of anonymous letters is a person who has never learned that facing the truth and loving can go together. People like that cannot believe that they can come out openly and express opposition, and love at the same time. They cannot believe that they can openly say they disapprove of something and still love. This is because they do not believe that someone cannot like something *they* do and still love *them*, and they project this onto other people.

It took me a while to realize that the person who is my most severe face-to-face critic is often my best friend. I'm thinking of two friends, one of them a man and the other a woman. I can hardly ever remember seeing them when they have not pointed out something I did wrong or something I should do better; and through the years, I have come to know that it is because they love me so much. They don't want anything left in me that someone might criticize, and so they are constantly working on me because of their love.

Often those who love us best are those who know our faults and tell us, but at the same time, let us know they love us. This is a wonderful characteristic, and when you have it, you have a part of the kingdom of heaven within you.

Finally, *believe in and accept what the Bible calls "the grace of God."* Then we can love others when we do not love everything they do, and we can accept the love of others who do not always love everything we do. The phrase "the grace of God" is the biblical way of expressing the fact that God knows everything about us, and he still loves us. When you accept this grace of God, it enables you to live it out with every other person with whom you are associated. The "grace of God" means he loves us, even though he knows everything about us, even that which we would let no other human being know.

A great Scottish evangelist said that after he was converted, the first person he wanted to witness to was his best friend. He went to him and said, "Ben, I came to talk to you about God." And his friend said, "I don't believe in God."

To this he answered, "Ben, I know you don't believe in God, but God believes in you, and I came to tell you about it. God knows you, but he still believes in you."

Very often in the Christian community, we have talked a lot about accepting God and, therefore, being saved. What is much more important is the knowledge that *God* accepts *us*.

One night when I was ten years old I had been to a revival meeting where the Reverend Dan Anders preached on the subject, "As the hart panteth after the water brook, so panteth my soul after Thee, O God."

As you know, the hart described in that Old Testament passage is a young deer, and I remember how Anders pictured the young deer in the forest. There is a forest fire and the deer has been running from the fire. The deer runs up on a little knoll to look around. He stands there panting, looking for a water brook.

And the evangelist said, "Just as that young deer stands there panting for the water brook, so pants my soul after thee, O God."

Something touched my life that night and, pushing past the other young people who were sitting in the pew with me, I stepped out into the aisle, went down to the altar, and gave the preacher my hand. I can tell you that I had never felt before and, I am sorry to say, never afterward, the beautiful feeling that came that night as I said to Brother Anders, "I want to accept God in my life."

He was an elderly man with long gray hair. He took my hand and patted it and said, "Son, that's wonderful that you are accepting God, and I'm so glad to tell you tonight that God accepts you."

God know all about you, but he loves you, and he's ready to give the same kind of love to all of us.

That's the Good News of the gospel!

PRAYER

Heavenly Father, we are so caught up these days in the escape mechanism of a religion of other worlds. We look up at the traffic light, and there pasted on the bumper of the car ahead of us are such words as, "Listen for the shout, He's coming again" or "In case of rapture, this car will be without a driver." These are symbols of a desire to escape the battle, longing for the day when the battle will be over. Father, help us to stop and think, that this is the best world you could possibly make and still give us free will.

Father, help us to understand that it is possible that we are to be saved in the midst of the battle, that it is not going to be over and that's what life is about . . . even eternal life—a constant struggle toward the light, the moving toward that goal at which we shall never arrive, the joy of new horizons every day in every life. Father, help us to see that the message of Jesus is not to save us out of this life. It is to save us in the midst of this life and that can best be done by the ability to love a person without loving everything a person does, to accept people's love without expecting them to like everything we do. Father, we believe this message has a miracle potential in every life. We thank thee in Jesus' name. Amen.

LOVE IS A
MANY-SPLENDORED THING

*T*hrough the years, my wife and I have gone to a good many Valentine parties and dinners, and we have enjoyed them very much. Two things have always interested me. One is the many jokes told about married love, which you always hear on such occasions when husbands and wives are together. It is always interesting to me that love, before you are married, is considered such a sacred and beautiful thing, and then immediately after you are married, it becomes something to tell jokes about.

The other is that on each of these Valentine occasions, there has been that moment of warmth and tenderness, when suddenly the group is enveloped by the realization that underneath all the good humor, there is a strong golden cord that ties us together.

One night we were attending one of those parties and singing some of the old love songs. Then the only soloist in the group began singing a song that was new to me. I don't remember all the words, but the song contained the phrase, "Love is a many-splendored thing." Immediately I began to think, "How true it is."

I thought of a diamond—a cut diamond—one that you might hold in your hand under a light to inspect; you turn it slowly one way and the other, and each time you turn it even the slightest bit, there is a new splendor, a new radiance about it. There are many facets to the beauty of a cut diamond, and this is the way it is with love—love is a many-splendored thing. Any quality or any degree of love radiates splendor to many different people in many different ways.

First, *love has much splendor for the one who is loved.* Any experience of love casts a radiance in the heart and mind of the person who is the recipient of that love—the loved person!

Of course, we never outgrow the need for love and affection. But this is especially true of the very young. The greatest single thing we do for the young is to love them. This equips them for life. In fact, if children are not properly loved by a mother and father, then they are not properly equipped for life. Later on they are incapable of the true quality of love.

There is a period of life when the greatest need of a human being is to be loved. The heart and soul must be poured full of love during this period, and unless this is done, that soul finds itself barren, in later years, of the ability to pour out love upon other people. There are exceptions, of course, but in the main, love must be given to children if they are to be successful in their experiences of love later on. Love seems to enable a child to give out love to others during the rest of life. Jesus said it this way, "Love one another, *as I have loved you.*" The mother or the father says to the child, "Now, go love others, as we have loved you," and this is a very necessary part of the training of a child.

There is a mistaken idea among many that you can love someone too much. One day I was talking to a family about some difficulty they were having with a teenage boy, and the mother said, "Dr. Dykes, the truth is, we have loved him too much."

This is a mistaken idea; you cannot love too much. There is no such thing as too much love. We can be too indulgent; we can be too lazy or selfish ourselves to properly discipline a child, but we cannot love too much. Love is something of which the more you have, the more beautiful your relationship becomes, and the more understanding there is between two people, the more the recipient of that love benefits by that experience.

More people have been saved by love than by any other one thing. Every now and then someone will ask a minister, "What can I do to save my husband—or my wife, or my daughter, my son, or my friend?" The greatest thing you can do is to love them. Love heals, strengthens, calms, encourages, and clarifies issues. The greatest single thing we can do for people, no matter what our goal for them may be, is to love them. If you have persons in mind for whom you would like to accomplish something good, your greatest single tool is to love them. Make them the recipient of your love, because to those who are loved, it is a splendid thing.

Second, *love has much splendor for the one who loves.* Our human need always demands that someone love us. But as we mature we also have the need *to* love.

If we have been loved properly up to a certain point in life, we become equipped, and our greatest need then is not just to *be* loved, but to love. The mark of truly mature persons is to reach the point where they not only have this need to *be* loved, but their need changes to wanting to love. There is a song entitled "My Task," and one line goes like this: "To love someone more dearly every day, this is my task."

It is not only our task; it is our privilege and our salvation. The sad person is one who is incapable of love—that is, one who, because of being frustrated in love, begins to hate, fear, and even murder. Adults who cannot find someone to surrender themselves to in love—not only romantic love, but in the true quality of Christian love—are sad people indeed. Love holds great splendor *for the lover*—that is, the person who gives the love. Everything good for us comes from that quality of loving.

Some time ago there was a person who came to our church. He was without a doubt the most unlovable person I think I have ever met. He chanced upon our church because of its location at the head of the downtown street. We have had many such people come for help, and I don't know why, but the first time he came into my office and began to tell his story, I thought to myself, "Why don't you try out love on this person, complete love, see what love can do—is anyone outside the power of love?"

So those of us on the church staff began an experiment and we spent, I suppose, a dispropor-tionate amount of time with that man. Some folks began to think we spent too much time with him, but they didn't know about our experiment in love. One of the wonderful things that came out of it was to watch him slowly soften under the influence of love. But that wasn't all. The surprising thing was to see what that effort did for us, as we tried to see how far we could go in loving. One of the splendid things about love is what it does for the person who tries it.

Third, *love also has a great splendor for those who witness it*. It has a splendor not only for those who receive it and for those who give it, but even for those who witness it.

One evening my wife and I watched a late movie, one of the old love stories. Of course we knew this was just a movie, but we were viewing a beautiful story of great love, and suddenly it got to me. Now, I don't even have to look at Sue to know when there is a lump in her throat and tears in her eyes. I've lived with her long enough that I just know. And I had a lump in my throat and tears in my eyes as we sat there together and viewed an experience of great love. Just to observe great love is a splendid thing. This is the reason so many stories and so many movies are on the theme of love.

But one of the greatest opportunities to observe love is the way children observe love between their parents, one for the other. The greatest single thing mother and daddy can do for the children is to love each other. The greatest security any child ever has is the security of the belief that mother and daddy love each other. The greatest cause of insecurity in a child is the belief, or even the suspicion, that mother and daddy do not truly love each other.

Some time ago a little boy came to my office crying and sobbing and catching his breath between sobs. He was about eight years old, and he told the story of an argument his mother and daddy had had at the breakfast table. I am sure they had soon made up, but he was possibly injured for life. The security of mother and daddy's love had been shaken.

This is also true of people who watch Christians. As members of a Christian church, the greatest single thing we could do for any community of which we are a part is to love one another, to let that community observe Christian love among people. The thing that hurts a church more than any other one thing is for people to get the impression that the members may not love one another, and especially if the impression is given that some dislike the others. Of all the effort in the name of Christ in a community, the greatest is to give the opportunity to observe, among us true Christians, love for one another.

Then the fourth splendor of love is that *it has splendor for all, even those who do not view it or observe it.* Any experience of love adds to the atmosphere of love in the world, and even those who do not know of this love or observe it will benefit by it. If you love someone very deeply, I may not ever know it or see it, but I benefit by it.

There are many who believe that when the atmosphere of love becomes strong enough in this world, all evil will be overcome and that even that which injures the body, as well as the mind and the soul, will be lessened. There are those who go so far as to believe that when there is enough atmosphere of love created in the world, evil will be so counteracted that even the damages and tragedies of nature, such as storms and cyclones, will cease to be. I do not know. But I do know that every time you love someone, you bring the kingdom of God a little closer upon the face of the earth.

There is only one power that will defeat evil in the world, and that is the power of love, and I believe it eventually will.

And finally, *love has splendor because it is of God.* "God is love." Anywhere love is, there God is, and no love is ever wasted. The way to bring God to a person is to bring love to that person.

I have so often seen a wife who, through the years, has wanted her husband to be converted to the Christian faith, has wanted him to be a part of the church, has wanted him to love God and give his heart to Christ. I have watched as she worked, prodded, and begged, concerning the church. Then finally she gave up all attempts to persuade and just quietly loved. Often this does it. When everything else fails, quiet, persistent love brings God into that life, because God is love, and wherever you bring love, you bring God.

If we are to bring God to our community, and especially to our fellowship of Christians, then the way to do it is to love one another. It beats all the sermons, it beats all the Sunday school lessons, it beats all the arguments and the publicity. The way to bring God is to bring love for one another.

"There abideth faith, hope, and love; but the greatest of all is love."

PRAYER

Our Heavenly Father, there are many things most of us cannot do. Some of us cannot sing, some of us cannot make a speech, some of us cannot express in words what we'd like to say. Some of us cannot go places or give money as we'd like to, and many times we wonder what we can do to bring the Kingdom. What we can do seems so insignificant and so small, and this world is so large, its problems are so complex, and evil is so powerful. What can I do?

Father, help us to see that the one thing that every person, even those with the most handicaps, can do is to love. And in the final analysis, it is the most powerful of all the things we can do.

May we project this splendid thing into every moment of our lives. And may we find it truly a many-splendored thing, for it is in Jesus' name, he who taught us perfect love, that we ask these blessings. Amen.

IS LOVE ALWAYS THE ANSWER?

On a special occasion, I had the opportunity to speak to the lay people and ministers of a church conference as they gathered on the campus of Lambuth College in Jackson, Tennessee.

There was one man there whom I had very much wanted to get to know personally. He occupies a rather unique and crucial position in the church today, a position that can do a great deal of good, and possibly some harm, unless it is handled carefully. So I looked for an opportunity to visit with him.

Finally, one evening after everything was over, he and I got together in his hotel room. We visited until well past midnight. I came to have a deep appreciation for him—his dedication, his strength, the enthusiasm with which he had undertaken his responsibilities, and his great desire to do that which is right. As we began to realize that we had to get to bed if we were going to get up and take part in the program the next morning, our conversation began to draw to a close.

I said to him, "Well, of course, we all realize that love is the answer to all of our problems."

He said, "I don't know. Evil is a very real thing in the world today and there are some situations that love just can't handle. To love, we must add justice."

I went back to my room and lay awake, thinking of our conversation. I could not help feeling we should have continued our conversation. Then I realized that he may have been much more realistic than I. Maybe I was using a phrase that sounded good, one that we had been accustomed to using but not really believing in at all. It seemed to me that maybe he was expressing one of the basic ideas that underlies the decisions most of us make most of the time. That is, that love is not always the answer; that love is the answer only up to a point, then finally there comes a time when it needs a little boost to get things done and accomplish its purpose. In some situations love is not enough. It needs some help. This is a very common idea.

A little boy came home from across the street after having a fuss with his best friend. He was miserable and moped around the kitchen with his mother and father. He wanted to be with his friend but they could not seem to get together.

The father could see how miserable the boy was and finally he said, "Son, why don't you try love and forgiveness? Go over there and say, 'Jimmy, we are friends and I love you, and I believe our friendship is bigger than our differences, and I just came over here to tell you I want to work them out.' "

The little boy said, "All right." So he got up and went to the door and turned around and said, "Daddy, I'm gonna do just exactly what you said, and then if he doesn't come around, I'm gonna knock his block off."

This is how we sometimes feel about love. We prefer to use love, but if it doesn't accomplish our purpose, we will resort to whatever method will make it work. This is one of the basic ideas upon which most human decisions are made at the personal, social, and national levels today. It is an idea that need serious rethinking. Our hero is not the one who takes and takes and takes again. Our hero is the one who takes and takes and takes, and then kills. No, our hero is not the one who continues to take; he's the one who takes long enough to demonstrate that he would rather deal in love, but if necessary, he has more of the other kind of strength than his enemy does.

Androcles and the Lion is a well-known play by George Bernard Shaw. The movie version of it shows the hero as a pacifist all during the story. But toward the end of the movie the pacifist surrenders his pacifism in the Roman arena, and then he does more killing than anyone else. The idea here is that love is best and is preferred, but sometimes it needs a little help. As Christians, we believe that love is the preferred answer but *not always the best*. In the passage "Love never fails," the biblical evidence is that love is the strongest force in the world.

The Scripture says, "God is love," and then on almost every page it says, "God is powerful." There is no power greater than God, and God is love. The Scripture asks that if God be for us, who can be against us? God is love.

First, is the answer to *family problems* always love? I mention this first because there are so many family problems. The number and seriousness of family problems are a daily amazement to me. I am constantly amazed at the extent and tragedy of unhappiness and the problems of people who live together in the same house. Most people would be relatively happy if they could get this part of their lives worked out.

I used to think that the greatest problem in marriage was unfaithfulness on the part of one of the partners. This is not true. In fact, infidelity is responsible for very few family breakups. I have seen infidelity forgiven many times, but the thing that has destroyed the family is the absence of the little daily evidences of love. Time and time again people forgive unfaithfulness, but the thing they cannot take is the absence of the little everyday actions that demonstrate a deep, abiding, warm quality of love. Of course, this does not excuse infidelity, and infidelity normally does not occur until there is a lack, to some extent at least, of this daily kind of love. The deadly lack of daily demonstrations of love is what destroys the family—the inability to say, by the way we act, "I love you." Love is the answer to every family problem.

One time a couple came to me for counseling. The man was the kind of fellow who might be called a real he-man. He said, "I am to blame; I take all the blame," then he began to outline his escapades. He was brazen and tough-shelled about it. He took on an air that said, "This is my privilege, and if she doesn't like it then she can get out, or I'll leave. I've got what it takes to get out, if that's what she wants."

Then almost inaudibly, his wife said, "Dr. Dykes, I still love him." He heard her, and I could almost visibly see his shell begin to crack. If she had been abusive, and accusing, and self-pitying, it is almost certain that the shell would have gotten thicker. But when that quiet voice that he had heard so often for so many years said, "I still love him," he began to melt.

Now, there may be some family problems beyond solution in this life, there may be some people who are impossible to live with, but let me say this: If there *is* a solution, love is it. In any situation in a family, if there *is* a solution or if there *is* an answer, then love is that answer.

Second, is the answer to our *social problems* always love? Let me say first of all that there are some social problems and injustices these days that are almost unbelievable, and any person who cannot see them is not looking, or seeing, very clearly. But none of these social problems has gone on long enough or is bad enough to demand the abandonment of the remedy of love.

I was talking with a group not long ago, and in the group was a man who represents a greatly oppressed segment of people in our society. They are people who have suffered great injustices. In talking about the methods to be used in trying to remove some of those abuses, he said with some impatience, "We have waited more than a hundred years!"

I could understand his feelings, but I should have said to him that God has waited two thousand years, and if it is necessary to wait for love to solve these injustices, then God will wait another thousand years. God never waits too long, nor is the situation ever bad enough for the abandonment of love. The time never comes when love can't quite make it unless it is helped along by some other power that can force its success.

There is never a time when we should say we can't wait any longer; we should simply wait until love is successful.

These are complicated times. Many of us are honestly asking, "What is right to do?" The answer, I believe, is that anything you and I can do out of love is right. But when resentment or hate or similar emotions become a tool to get the desired results, then maybe we must wait another hundred years.

"Social" also applies to personal relationships with groups at the office or in the neighborhood. Have you ever seen a spite fence? I was driving through a community some time ago, and in the midst of this subdivision was a spite fence. It was as plain as if there had been a sign on it. Between two little bungalows was a fence higher than the top of either of the houses. It was made of solid board and painted one color on one side and another color on the other. I didn't know the occupants, but I felt so sorry for those people who lived on either side of that fence. Don't ever build a spite fence.

The answer to any human difference at the personal social level is love. "Love your neighbor. Do good to those that spitefully use you." It is amazing how many people do not speak to their neighbors. And if they do speak because they feel they must be civil, their words are like icicles hanging on the fence.

Some time ago I had the temptation to build a spite fence, but not one against my neighbors, not one made of boards. This was a different kind of spite fence. This was a kind that finally said, "All right, I can do without him. I can get along without him; I don't have to be on good terms with him. We don't see alike.

Let him go his way; I will go mine. I'll make it." I was about to build the spite fence.

My wife said, "Why don't we make an experiment and pray for these people by name?" So we got on our knees that night, and it came my turn to pray, and suddenly I was surprised. I had prayed for these people before, but I was surprised how difficult it was now to call their names aloud in prayer. We need to call the name of our neighbor in prayer. We must love our neighbor. There are some people, maybe, you feel you can't get along with in this life; but let me say that if there is an answer, love is it. Nothing else has the power of love.

Then, is love always the answer to *national and international problems?* Politicians so often try to demonstrate that they are prepared to take a tougher stand against an enemy than their political opponents take. They all try to say that they hate the enemy more than their opponents do. It may not be stated in those words, but this is the idea: "I dislike the enemy more than my opponent does; therefore I should be elected." This is in line with the way we think, and it very likely goes a long way in getting someone elected.

A candidate would be a fool to pitch a campaign on the slogan, "I love communists more than my opponent does. I love the enemy more than my opponent does." But that is biblical. That is Christian. The Scripture says, "Love your enemy," and according to Scripture, the person who comes nearest to the solution would be the one who could demonstrate more love for the enemy than the opponent has.

George Bernard Shaw, on one occasion, said,

"There is much good in the Christian religion and the teachings of Jesus, but no nation would allow it to be practiced." Was he right? This kind of loving is not achieved by just deciding we are going to love. A man says, "Well, I'm going to love my family so much that I am going to solve our problems" or "I am going to start loving my neighbor and I'm going to take down the fence." You don't achieve love this way just by making the decision.

The only way you can love this way is by being totally reborn and rebuilt from within—that is, by what our ancestors called salvation through Jesus Christ. Up until then, this kind of love does not make sense really. If and when you or I *are* rejuvenated in this fashion and reborn to this kind of love, the world will not understand it. And *we* will not understand it until we have this rebirth.

This is the reason that when Nicodemus came asking about the things he just couldn't understand in the teachings of Jesus, Jesus said very simply in order for him to understand, "Nicodemus, you must be born again." You have to be totally remade in order to be able to love this way. This kind of loving comes only by that personal experience with Jesus Christ which converts and remakes the human soul. Then you can say with Saint Paul, "The things I once hated I now love, and the things I once loved, I now hate. I can do all things through Christ who strengtheneth me." This is true, because, you see, *love never fails.*

PRAYER

O Lord, our Heavenly Father, so often it seems that the principles of Jesus hang in the balance. We believe in Jesus, we admire him, we read of him with warmth and satisfaction. Yet, Heavenly Father, there seem to be some serious questions in our minds as to the practicability of some of his teachings. Is love always the answer? Father, if it is not, then give some kind of revelation greater than Jesus, because we search in vain for any evidence other than this, in what he says and what he did. Father, if love is always the answer, then help us to find that strength in him, because we have a feeling that, in a very real way, the world as we know it, and certainly our little personal worlds, so often hang in the balance, determined by what we really believe about this question. Help us to see as in the light of eternity. These blessings we ask in his name. Amen.

FAITHFUL TO ONE;
LOVE ANOTHER

O ne Saturday morning about 11:00 while I was in the study preparing my sermon, Selwyn Roberts, one of our college students who was working at the reception desk, called me on the phone and told me a young lady was downstairs asking for me.

I didn't remember any appointment at that particular time, and I quickly checked my secretary's date book, but I couldn't find the name listed, so I was a little hesitant.

Very often on such Saturdays, when people show up unexpectedly and drop in in this fashion, they usually are transient people looking for a cash handout. I always find it difficult to tell them no, and of course we cannot give money to all who come.

But I told Selwyn that if he would have her take a seat in one of the offices downstairs, I would be there in a few minutes. I finished the paragraph I was writing on the sermon and then went down. When I walked in, there was a beautiful young woman about twenty years of age, extremely well-dressed and fashionable. She was obviously not a transient looking for a cash handout.

She introduced herself, and when we were seated she apologized for coming without an appointment but said she felt she must talk to someone.

Immediately she said, "Dr. Dykes, is it possible to love two people at one time?"

Now the answer to her question is both yes and no, but it is an extremely important question. In fact, learning the answer to this particular question is possibly the single most important thing a person ever learns about living this life happily. The complex problem in answering that particular question arises out of the fact that there are several kinds of love. In one of these kinds of love, the answer is a definite "No, you cannot love two people at one time"; but in all the rest of the kinds of love, the answer is a definite *yes*. In fact, in all the rest, it is absolutely necessary for us to be able to love more than one person at a time.

Understanding the different kinds of love is essential if a person is going to answer the question concerning his or her life. The Greeks have four words for love; in English we have only one. That one word must serve in expressing any experience or any emotion we have in this general category of love.

William Barclay, that delightful theologian who for twenty-seven years taught in the University of Glasgow in Scotland, and whose Bible study books have sold more than a million copies, says, in discussing the kinds of love, that if a man speaks Gaelic, he can tell a girl he loves her in nineteen different ways, but the English have only one way. At the time of the writing of the thirteenth chapter of First

Corinthians by Paul, the Greeks had four words for love.

First, there was *eros*. This kind of love always has to do with sex. It is always the love of a man for a woman or a woman for a man. This word does not appear in the New Testament, and Barclay says it is not because the New Testament does not believe in physical love, but because by the time the New Testament was written, the word *eros* had become the word for *lust*, rather than love.

The second Greek word for love is *philia*. *Philia* is the word for real affection, affection for a friend or a neighbor or a co-worker, or even affection for your dog. *Philia* involves the warm outgoing of personality which expresses itself in a firm handshake or a hug or just walking in and sitting down in the room with a friend who is in trouble. This is one of the highest forms of love.

The third word is *storgé*, and this is family love. It is the love of a brother for his sister. This is the love of a son for his mother. This is the love of a father for his daughter. There is no sex in this kind of love—family love.

In the writing of the thirteenth chapter of First Corinthians by Paul, none of these three words is used—not *eros*, not *philia*, not *storgé*. He uses a fourth, totally different word. It is interesting to note that the word he uses does not appear in any Greek writing before the New Testament. The verb is used previously, but not the noun. That word is *agape*. It is a completely new word for a completely new kind of love introduced in the time of Jesus.

Now this fourth kind of love is expressed first in the closing verses of the fifth chapter of Matthew, in the very midst of the Sermon on the Mount. Jesus says, "God sends his rain on the just and the unjust. God makes his sun to shine on the evil and on the good." That is to say, no matter whether you are good or bad or indifferent, God still sends his gifts to you. In other words, nothing you can do, nothing you can be, will stop God from loving you. Again in the words of William Barclay, "Be what you like, do what you like, God continues to offer us all the free beauty of his gifts."

Now that is what *agape* is; that is what Christian love is—the undefeatable, unceasing attitude of goodwill. Christian love means that no matter what the other person does, we will never, at any time, do anything but seek that person's highest good. We will never do anything except in that person's interest.

Now of all these four kinds of love, there is only one for which the answer to the young woman's question is "No, you can't love two people at one time," and that love is called *eros*. In fact, if you try to love more than one person at a time, *eros* escapes you completely, and the extent to which you are able to love only one is the extent to which you discover the deepest meaning and satisfaction of *eros*.

The playboy who is determined to squeeze everything out of *eros* by loving many women will find that *eros* eventually escapes him completely. In fact, he starts by trying sex with many partners. Then he tries many variations of sex with many partners, only to ultimately find that no one and nothing satisfies him at all. This is the reason that often the man who starts as a playboy winds up totally frustrated and even "turned-off" by sex, and the girl who decides to experiment outside the total commitment to one person often finds herself unable to love anyone.

The pure joy that a totally committed couple knows in the physical presence and touch of each other is the greatest of all relationships between a man and a woman. In the kind of love expressed in the Greek word *eros*, the answer to the question, "Can you love more than one person at a time?" is an unqualified *no*. But the answer to the question in the other three kinds of love is *yes*. You *must* be able to love more than one person at a time.

First, *there is philia*. *Philia* is the word for true affection. It is the affection we feel for a friend or a neighbor, or a co-worker in a common goal. It's the kind of support and cooperation between people who share common interests, tasks, or goals, and who share common joys and sorrows. This kind of love is expressed in a beautiful poem:

> I love you not only for what you are
> But for what I am when I am with you.

In *philia*, we must understand that this kind of love is not limited. We can be faithful to one and still love another. People make a great mistake when they are jealous of a friend. Jealousy is one of the most miserable and destructive of all human emotions, and all jealousy has its roots in the misbelief that love between friends somehow is limited. We sometimes feel that if a friend we love or a friend we want to love us demonstrates love for another person, that automatically threatens the love the friend has for us. This comes out of a lack of understanding of the nature of *philia* love. *Philia* must be shared to be healthy. Every person your friend loves enables him or her to love you more. We don't have to cast off an old friend to love a new one, and we should never assume that we have lost a friend when that friend discovers a new one.

Some of us apparently feel sometimes that we are showing loyalty to one person when we refuse to accept another person. The truth is that the people who are most capable of being true friends are always giving themselves to more and more people. I have a friend who bothers me a little. I love him, but when I am with him, he often seems to feel he can show his friendship for me best by downgrading others and comparing me favorably to them. I find myself often wondering what he will say about me when he finds a new person to be his friend. Don't ever feel you can't love a new friend without being unfaithful to an old one.

Now, second, *we can love more than one person at a time in the love called storgé*—that is, family love. When the young wife is jealous of her mother-in-law, when the mother is jealous of her son's wife, or when the younger brother is jealous of his elder brother, they are missing the truth entirely and are experiencing misery that is totally unnecessary. It may be natural for a little child to be possessive and feel threatened when a new baby is born in a home where the first child has been the only child and received all the attention.

My wife and I went to a General Conference of The United Methodist Church. When we got on the plane to come home, next to us in the window seat was a young woman with a little boy about three years old. It was a long flight, and he became restless. In fact, it was a little difficult to keep him in his seat at times, but finally he wore down. I looked over, and he had fallen asleep with his head on my wife's shoulder.

A few days after we got home, our granddaughter, who is four years old, came to see us, and my wife thought it would be very good to tell her this little experience. And so she told her about this little boy who was on the plane with us and all the things he did, and then she said, "He finally put his head on my shoulder and went to sleep."

Suddenly our little granddaughter looked up and said, "Did you tell him you're *my* grandmother?"

But the mark of true maturity is to know that with the beautiful kind of love the Greeks call *storgé*, you can be faithful to one and love another, and a family that doesn't know this is in for trouble.

Now, *the third and final kind of love in which we must be able to love more than one person at a time is agape. Agape* is that active goodwill toward all people, known in Christian circles as *unconditional love.*

This answers the question many people ask: "How can I love my enemy the same way I love my wife or child, my son, or my daughter, or my friend?" The answer is that you are not asked to love your enemy in the same way you love these. It's a different kind of love. This *agape,* this Christian love, means you can *love* when you don't *like.* Even when a person wrongs us or hurts us or injures us, we can still keep up this attitude of absolute, undefeatable, never-ending goodwill, and that is Christian love.

Agape says that you and I can never do anything to

people that is not in their best interest, no matter what they have done to us. Now of course this kind of love is obviously not something that is only a response of the heart. William Barclay says we speak of falling in love as if it were like stepping on a banana peel—you step on it and away you go. You are "in love."

But Christian love, this *agape*, is an effort. It involves the total personality. It is an exercise of the will; it's a great victory. It is the victory of loving a person you don't like. It is loving the unlovable; it's loving the unlikable.

I'm convinced that *agape* is the root foundation of all other kinds of love. You can't have real joy and satisfaction in *eros* or *philia* or *storgé* if you cannot first have *agape* for that person. You cannot have sexual love or friend love or family love unless you first have *agape*. All the people you love in any other way at some times are unlikable, and unless you have *agape* for them, you cannot have any other kind of love for them. And so, when a Christian loves all humankind, every living human being, with *agape*, this makes possible all the rest. This is the central message of the Christian faith.

PRAYER

Father, of all the subjects in the world today, possibly we are more confused about love than about any other. Help us in the midst of all our talk about love to sort it out in the light of this beautiful thirteenth chapter of First Corinthians—the New Testament kind of love—Jesus' kind of love. In his name we ask it. Amen.

MALE AND FEMALE:
THE ART OF LOVING

*I*t has always been puzzling for Christians to find Christian principles being lived, and Christian philosophy being taught, by non-Christian people. This was true even in Bible times. You remember there was an occasion when the disciples heard some people teaching some of the same things they were teaching, and they were not doing it *in the name of Jesus.* So the disciples came to Jesus and told him about it: "Master, we stopped them from doing this because these are *our* principles of life." And Jesus said, "Don't stop them . . . those who are not against us are for us." So often in our experience we find Christian principles and Christian ideas among those who do not profess to be Christians.

I find this is true in my own attitude toward a beautiful philosophy concerning love written by Eric Fromm. I quote from him often. He has written that beautiful little book *The Art of Loving.* In the first chapter is probably one of the finest treatises on love in all of modern literature.

One of the main things he says in that chapter is that

love is an *art*. You have to learn it. You are not born knowing how to do it. He says that love is an art just as truly as playing a violin or a piano, and you have to learn to do these things. Even though you may have native talent, you have to be taught, you have to study, you have to learn to do them well.

We so often act as if we are born knowing how to love, and all we have to do is find the right person. We assume that to be the secret, when really that isn't the way it is at all. What really matters is whether or not you have the *capacity* to love unconditionally and properly. The person you marry is relatively unimportant compared to your capacity for love. This is the philosophy of Eric Fromm in *The Art of Loving*.

It's very interesting, also, that people can be so smart in other things and so "unsmart" in the art of loving. Many great surgeons, for example, are extremely skilled as surgeons and in the medical arts and have no idea how to love. Many teachers, lawyers, scientists, and others, are extremely intelligent and well educated, yet they don't know how to love.

I know a man who is one of the finest surgeons I've ever known and yet he escapes to the hospital or to his office because he never has learned how to love at home. His home is a miserable place—so miserable that he leaves and will hardly go there until everybody else is asleep, because he doesn't know how to love and be loved.

I know a businessman who can make a million dollars on one deal and has proved it a good many times, and yet when he is not in his office, he escapes to the golf course or to the country club to keep from going home, because he has never mastered the art of loving. This problem is not confined to any group or profession; it cuts across all segments of society.

The art of loving is the greatest lesson a person ever learns, and the interesting thing is that there are no courses in it in school. You would think that the most important thing a person ever learns would certainly have textbooks and courses in school to teach you how to love, but there are none. One of the great tragedies of our educational system is that it teaches us all the arts except the greatest art of all—the art of loving.

As I have mentioned before, my wife and I have two little granddaughters. I want them to learn a lot of things. But I would rather they would learn how to love properly than learn anything else in the world.

Now, I would like for us to consider one particular love relationship—that is, love between a man and a woman who are married. This is the most comprehensive and all-encompassing kind of love. It is the only love relationship in which all the kinds of love can and must be present.

We have talked about the different kinds of love and the different words for love in the Greek language— *eros,* meaning passionate love; *philia,* meaning friendship love; *storgé,* meaning family love; and *agape,* meaning unconditional goodwill—that is, Christian love. The relationship between a husband and a wife is the only human relationship in which all these kinds of love must be present. In the other relationships of love between human beings, it would be strange—in fact, abnormal if all these were present in the same relationship.

Marriage is *communication.* When you have communication, you can keep your marriage. When you lose it, you have lost your marriage, even though you may continue to live in the same house. Love depends upon communication, and love must be expressed. Let's consider some of the levels of communication between a man and a woman who love each other and live together.

First of all, there is *physical communication*. This is the communication of touch, and it is extremely important.

One of the most important things parents can teach their children is to be able to communicate by touch. Occasionally after Sunday morning worship when I am speaking to people and shaking hands, some people will pull their hand away quickly. They can hardly stand for anyone to touch them. I always feel sorry for those people. They have never learned to receive and to communicate love in a touch.

In the case of a man and a woman who are married, this communication is of a very intimate nature. They must be able to give themselves physically. And they must be able to receive the other person physically. This is sexual communication—physical touch of the most intimate nature. It's sad when people married to each other are embarrassed by physical communication. The husband who cannot openly receive the most intimate touch of his wife, the wife who cannot receive the most intimate touch of her husband— these people are in for trouble.

It is extremely unfortunate that very early in the history of the church, the impression was gained that sex, the most intimate physical communication, is evil. Probably a misinterpretation of the book of Genesis is most responsible for this, because somehow the serpent, the apple, and the Garden of Eden have become associated with physical intimacy.

The passage of Scripture, "In sin my mother conceived me," expresses this idea. It was believed that babies were born in sin, and the church believed and taught that they had to be cleansed by baptism. They were born doomed to hell because they were born as a result of physical intimacy between a man and a woman. The whole concept of the virgin birth and its great significance in the early days of the church may have sprung out of this misconception, because they did not understand that the physical intimacy of a man and a woman is one of the most beautiful and holy things in all of God's creation.

Any couple that has difficulty in this area of their marriage should get help from some professional person early in their relationship. It is amazing how long disappointment and dissatisfaction can go on between a man and a woman when they really love each other but do not have a truly satisfactory physical communication. The ultimate in physical communication is what the Scripture calls "becoming one"—the total physical surrender to each other.

Now I must not close this point without stating very strongly that this kind of love is extremely important, but it cannot exist alone. One of the greatest problems of marriage today is that this physical communication is sometimes the only kind of love a young man and woman feel they need. But it cannot exist alone.

Second, for love to exist in marriage, there also must be *social communication,* being together with pleasure when you are *not* touching. This is what has been called "liking as well as loving"—doing things together, having common interests and mutual friends. It's what one of the old popular songs called catching each other's eye "across a crowded room," that communication which takes place between a man and a woman, even when they may be in a group, sitting across the room from each other.

All husbands and wives should have time together *with* the rest of the family and *without* the rest of the family. Every husband and wife should have at least one date a week in which the children are not involved. They should be alone together. They should do something together socially, even if it's no more than a walk in the woods, or calling on grandmother, or taking a ride, or sitting on the back porch alone together. There should be some regular, social communication between a husband and a wife.

When some man says to me, "We can't afford a trip together," I say to him, "The truth is, you can't afford *not* to have a trip together." You must develop some common interests: grow flowers together, read together, do community service together, do church activities together, build something together, develop mutual friends. I'm always concerned when I say to some wife, "What about your social communication?" and she says, "Well, he has his interests and friends, and I have mine." This is the making of trouble. We must respect and like each other's friends. But social communication alone together, or with friends, is extremely important between two people who live together.

Then third, there is *intellectual communication.* This is the ability to know what the other person *thinks,* the ability to talk about ideas. It is the ability to talk about things other than car payments and new shoes for the children or what the neighbors are doing.

This is the reason educational background is so important. Some months ago, a young man who has a Ph.D. came to my office. He teaches at a university. He had fallen very much in love with a young woman who was an exotic dancer in a local night club. She quit school in the fifth grade. She was beautiful. I could understand how he could fall in love with her.

After talking with them a few minutes, I separated them and talked with each of them alone. Both of them said, "It doesn't really matter. We love each other so much." They thought that what they felt for each other would overcome all handicaps. Maybe a true love can, but they will have many a hard time ahead of them. Educational background is important, because intellectual communication often depends upon it.

Finally, there is *spiritual communication*, knowing what the other person *feels*. This is the level of communication many people *never* have. In fact, many don't even *know* about it. It is amazing how many people live together for ten, twenty, or thirty years and never really know each other.

So often through the years I will be counseling with a husband or a wife and she (if it is the wife) will tell me something she feels very deeply about, and I say, "Does your husband know you feel this way?" And I guess I have heard it a thousand times—"Oh no, I couldn't tell him, he wouldn't understand." They *live* together, they *eat* together, they *sleep* together, but they don't really know each other.

This is the major trouble in marriages today. It's not that anyone wants to hurt anyone else. The vast majority of people do not want to hurt anyone, especially someone they are married to. They just don't *know* each other spiritually.

To live together with someone as closely as a husband and wife do, and really know each other, is the nearest thing to heaven on earth. It is the greatest of all human experiences. But to live that intimately and *not* really know each other, always be guessing and wondering "why she said that" or "why he did what he did" is hell, and not many people can stand it for a lifetime. Often *this* is what causes the breakup of marriages—a lack of spiritual communication.

Now we close with a bit of advice on spiritual communication which I give to all couples before I perform the ceremony. I say to them:

"On the very first day of your marriage, when the ceremony is over—when everybody has congratulated you and you get in your car to go to whatever place you have chosen—when you get to that place and close the door on the privacy of your marriage for the first time—get down on your knees, take each other by the hand, and each of you, *aloud in the presence of the other*, offer a prayer. It need not be a planned prayer or a formal prayer. It may be as simple as 'Lord, bless our marriage and help me to be a good wife' or 'Lord, bless our marriage and help me to be a good husband.' Even if it is as simple as this, it will be bowing in God's direction from the very beginning, and it will do more for the success of your marriage than anything else you can do.

"The reason I say do this the very first day is that if you do not pray together the first day, it will be more difficult to do on the second, and harder the third, and it is very likely that if you don't pray together the first day, you never will. But if you do so the first day, it will be easier the second, the third, and the fourth day, until in a very brief time it will be as natural and as easy as eating breakfast together. Nothing will guarantee your happiness and make your dreams come true more than this.

"Then when you are back from whatever honeymoon you planned and settle into the routine of life, *add to* the prayer time. At the close of the day when the dinner dishes are washed and the cat is put out and you have your pajamas on and the world is shut out for the day, take your Bible and take turns (one one night and the other the next) and read a little in it. Read enough to get an idea or a story or a parable, then sit and talk about the passage.

"Say, 'What do you think that means?' or 'I've always thought it means so and so' or 'It sounds like it means so and so' or 'Read it again. I didn't get it.'

"Discuss one or more of the great questions of life together, such as, 'What is life all about to you? What is your goal? When we are old and gray and sitting on the back porch together, what do you want life to have been?'

"Questions like 'What do you believe about God? When someone says *God* in your presence, what do you see? What about sin? Is there such a thing as sin? Do *you* sin? If we have sinned, how are we forgiven?'

"Questions like 'What is love? When someone says, I love you, what is he or she talking about? What is faithfulness? What does it mean to be faithful to someone you love? Is it something you don't do—or something you don't think—or something you don't feel?'

"Questions like 'What is salvation? What does it mean to be *saved?* Are *you* saved? What about death and heaven and hell—what do you believe about these things?'

"There are a hundred different questions, and the answers are programmed deep within us, out of which all of our decisions and responses come. Then after discussing one or more of these questions together, get on your knees and take each other by the hand and pray together, as you have done from the first day you were married. You do this one day—do it two—do it for a year—do it for ten years, and gradually you will draw a spiritual image of each other. You will know not only what he or she will do under any given circumstance, but you know *why* they do it."

This kind of spiritual communication comes primarily from talking *to* God together. It may be trite, but there is a lot of truth in the saying, "The family that *prays* together *stays* together."

PRAYER

Our Heavenly Father, we thank you so much for the fact that even though we are not born masters of the art of love, we are all born with the potential to learn and develop this, the greatest of all arts.

We pray that you will help us with the ability to have physical, social, intellectual, and spiritual communication with the one we have chosen as our life's mate. Be with us, Father, as we seek to master the art of loving. Amen.

SOME WAYS TO CREATE LOVE

*A*ll of us have wondered at times why it is that some people have such an ability to create love in others, while many of us have such a difficult time getting people to love and appreciate us. So often people who have that ability do not seem to be attractive in many ways, yet they have an intangible quality which inspires love and appreciation in the people about them.

There are certain things that will create that love. Before I list them, let me make two statements by way of introduction.

First, a few people do not have the ability to love anyone but themselves. They are incapable of love.

The other statement is that these ways I am about to suggest cannot be used selfishly. This is a very important point, because some people will go to any length to create love for themselves on the part of other people, without really loving the other people. They immediately lose their effectiveness.

It is not enough to know what is needed to paint a picture. It is not enough to know the instruments needed to create a work of art. Knowing the equipment or possessing the equipment to paint with does not ensure that you will produce a work of art. It takes more.

In other words, assuming that you love the person in whom you want to create a similar response, these things will work.

Let me say also that I shall mention Jesus in describing these things that produce love. He was the one who used them perfectly. The question might arise in your minds that if these are the ways that will produce love on the part of others and Jesus used them perfectly, why did it not create love in the people who crucified him? I think the answer is that the people who did that to Jesus did not know him. He was crucified either by people who had not had the opportunity to know him or by people who, like Judas, refused to know him. I cannot conceive of any person resisting the power of these methods as they were used by Jesus, if they allowed themselves to really know him personally.

The first way to create love is with *confidence and expectation.* People have a way of living up to, or down to, that which those who are supposed to love them expect of them. The people we want to love us and those we are supposed to love have a way of living up to whatever we expect of them. I have known it to happen so often that suspicion on the part of a marriage partner has created in the other the very thing the partner suspects.

I have in mind a young man who, I am thoroughly convinced, was faithful to his wife, but she constantly suspected him, questioned him, and watched him, until in a few years the time came when he began to doubt his love himself, he began to question his own faithfulness. And eventually, she had made him guilty of the very thing she had constantly suspected. We have a tendency to live up to, or down to, that which people who are supposed to love us expect.

We should have confidence in the love of other people. We should assume that people love us. It's a sad thing when we go about day after day, demanding proof that people love us. Some of the saddest people I ever meet are the people who must have constant proof of another's love—people who do not have confidence in someone's love.

A woman came to my office very distressed because her husband did not prove or demonstrate his love as regularly as she thought he should. Now the strange thing is that if she had confidence in his love, very likely he would have done so. The very fact of needing proof of love indicates that there is a question as to whether the love is there, and that question destroys love in the heart and mind of the other person.

There are a few things that will build love, such as confidence in that love and expectation of that love. In fact, a very good rule for creating love in other people is to do all we can to prove our own love, but never to require proof of another's love. We should assume that we are wanted. If you move into a community and begin to separate the people who want you from the people who don't want you, it won't be long until you'll wonder if anybody wants you. The way to create love in any circumstance is to assume that people want you, that you are welcome and that you are loved.

Look for the good in those you want to love you. Have confidence in the good. Especially in family circles, we ought to look for the good and point it out.

Take children, for instance. We who are parents ought to spend our time finding their good qualities and reminding them of those qualities. The world is going to do enough pointing out of the bad. I catch myself, and I expect you do too, spending a great deal of our conversation on the bad. There are enough people in the world who will constantly remind them of their bad qualities. We who are their parents ought to spend our time in that wonderful privilege of seeking, finding, and pointing out the good about them.

If enough people point out our weakness, that weakness becomes an obsession. Many a teenage boy has become more and more clumsy because everybody is pointing out how big his hands and feet are and how clumsy he is. Many a teenage girl has been loved into a lifelong devotion to her family because during a certain period her parents had shown that they believe in her good qualities, when all the world was acting as if she made nothing but mistakes. And we parents ought to do it not only for our children but for each other. The world outside is cruel enough about our faults. For the people we love, we ought to claim the privilege of finding their wonderful and good qualities. Confidence and expectation create love.

The second way to create love is with *forgiveness*. I am amazed at how unforgiving we are of those we love. Often we are more forgiving of other people than we are of the people we love most and those we want to love us. And that's strange, because we should be more forgiving with the people we love than with anyone else.

When the sinful woman broke the alabaster box and poured the contents over his head, and someone in the crowd pointed out her sinfulness, Jesus made this wonderful statement—"He that has been forgiven much, loves much." Forgiveness creates love.

Love often is more mature after a great forgiveness. Don't misunderstand this, but I have known situations in which there had been unfaithfulness in marriage on the part of one partner or both, and that unfaithfulness has been completely forgiven. In the process, a wonderful quality of love developed that had not been there before.

It's sad that it takes such an experience to create love. But complete forgiveness can do something good for love. Even that which is tragic can become a blessing if forgiveness takes over. This gives a kind of maturity, power, and beauty, which love that has not been tested often does not possess.

Forgive the people who love you, and don't let that forgiveness become difficult. Don't act as if you are being generous as you forgive. Just forgive easily. Some people are afraid to forgive easily because they think it encourages abuse—that if you forgive too easily, then people will be tempted to do the same thing again. That is not true. No one forgave as easily as Jesus, and no one inspired noble living as did Jesus. Easy forgiveness does not encourage abuse. Easy forgiveness brings out the highest and noblest qualities in a person.

The third way to create love is with *sacrifice and service*. People who have been *forced* by circumstances to sacrifice for each other have a special tenderness toward each other.

Two army buddies who have been forced to share their rations or their canteen of water in a difficult time never forget each other. There is something about sacrificing together that creates love.

I certainly do not encourage early marriage, but I do not think a couple ought to wait until no sacrifice is necessary. Do you remember the early days of your marriage, when you went through difficult times together? Do you remember when you had to sacrifice so your husband could have a new suit or your wife could have a new dress the same year? Those were loving years. In those years, foundations of permanent, eternal love were created. I feel sorry for people who have never had to sacrifice for each other. There is something about sacrifice that creates love.

There is a poem that says something like this: "Share with others your joys, but bring me your tears." When you share sacrifice with someone, it creates love. As I look back, I am deeply touched by the memory of the people who sacrificed for me, with no hope of profit to themselves. This creates love in the human heart.

Some time ago I preached a baccalaureate sermon at a graduation exercise, and one young woman, when she received her diploma, instead of going back to her seat, walked about halfway into the audience and laid the diploma in the lap of her mother. The mother looked a little tired, and her dress was not the latest style. I never knew the reason, but I suspect that girl was saying, "I know how you've sacrificed for me to be here tonight." It was a demonstration of love.

Now if you happen to be thinking, "I have loved someone and she didn't appreciate it" or "I have sacrificed for someone and he didn't appreciate it," let me suggest that the very fact that you think that is a fair indication that your sacrifice was not made in the right spirit. I doubt that the mother who had the diploma laid in her lap ever knew she was making a sacrifice. If we feel cheated in our sacrifice, we have loved selfishly.

The fourth way to create love is with *kindness and courtesy*. Occasionally a young woman comes to me with the question, "Should I marry this boy?" The young man, of course, never knows that she is asking this. I always question her: "Is he kind? Is he a kind man?" I think you can live with someone and overlook almost anything if that person is kind. Even though someone has a lot of qualities but is unkind, that ruins it.

I am amazed at the discourtesy of which we are capable toward the very people we want to love us. The lack of common courtesy toward the people we want to love us is one of the most detrimental things in the world.

Occasionally I see a couple who shout at each other. And sometimes they do it so long that it becomes a part of them, and they do it before their friends in public. And often you'll hear someone comment, "Oh, they understand each other." I always wonder . . . do they? Do you ever understand unkindness and discourtesy? Do we ever get to the place where we understand unkindness? I can't imagine tender love growing in such ground. Kindness and courtesy create love.

The fifth way to create love is with *patience*. I think sometimes that an even temper will come closer to gaining love and respect than anything else.

I was in a group not long ago, and we were talking about a person we all appreciate and love very much. And the main comment was this: "He's the same every time you meet him—never moody, never ill-tempered. He is always the same."

When I think of the people I appreciate most, I think that's the quality I appreciate in them. They are the same every time you meet them.

One burst of temper, one unkind word said in haste, can leave a scar on love that never disappears. If you want to create love in people, one of the simplest steps to take is to control your temper. And thank God, that's one thing we all *can* do!

"Love suffers long, and is kind; love envieth not; love vaunteth not itself, is not puffed up, doth not behave itself unseemly, seeketh not her own, is not easily provoked, thinketh no evil; rejoiceth not in iniquity, but rejoiceth in the truth; beareth all things. And *love never fails.*"

PRAYER

O Lord, our Heavenly Father, we realize that we love the people who have been patient, forgiving, kind, and sacrificial on our behalf. Even the thought of it puts a lump in our throats. Teach us, Heavenly Father, the effectiveness of these same characteristics in our love.

For it is in the name of the One who perfected love that we ask it, even Jesus. Amen.

With Deep Appreciation to
Kathryn Sue
and
David